PINK

SPACES BECOMING PLACES

PINK
Spaces becoming places

by
Leanne M Christie

leanne m christie
be a collector

2018

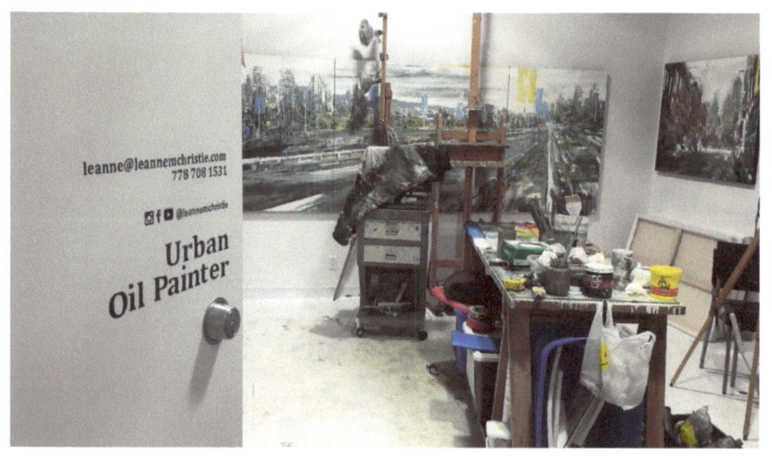

First Printing: 2018
ISBN 978-1-7750634-0-7

Leanne M Christie inc.
268 Keefer Street.
Studio 50
Vancouver, BC, V6A 1X5

www.leannemchristie.com

Contents

Index of paintings:

1. Preface

The reason I paint the urban is simple. When I paint the streets, I paint you.

This is the theatre of your life. The corner where you first tested your freedom and wandered further than you had before. The stretch of road where your exasperated mother pulled over as the back seat erupted with recriminations and retaliation. The house where you failed the ring and run trick. The store where your grandparents bumped into each other and the coffee shop where you caught each other's eye. The quiet avenue where your dad taught you to drive and your mom bravely allowed you to practice on her.

The urban is the space between and when it is transformed into place, it entwines with us and becomes the fabric of our memories and through the years, its familiarity is our open return ticket. The streets bear witness as the opaque veil of time descends.

I paint the city for the grand reason that this is who we are. I paint the city because it is not static. It is rich and evolving and it strives to be everything to everyone and in the process, places are lost.

I paint the city because I bear witness to the witness.

2. About Leanne M Christie

Urban Oil painter Leanne M Christie has a reputation for complex paintings, built with powerful brushwork and the sophisticated manipulation of white. She paints full time in her Vancouver studio and her daily 50km cycling commute from her home in Coquitlam, gives Christie an intimate kinship with the flow and stories of the urban streets. The unrehearsed transitory moments provide the abundant source of her paintings.

Born and raised in South Africa, Christie moved to the Canadian West Coast in the late 2000's after a period of 10 years abroad. A period that had originated as a 2 week holiday after the completion of her Bachelor of Fine Art from Rhodes University.

Christie's paintings are at first understood by the viewer whose participation is then demanded by her relentless harnessing of the communicative properties unique to oil painting. The distilled open relationship between the painter and the slow drying oils is the unique characteristic of the medium that Christie burrows into to activate the complexity that the alchemy of passive and active time develops. Active time is dependant on the relationship that the viewer develops with the work.

Christie's concept of complexity through the inclusion of active and passive time as a catalytic element in the paintings, finds the perfect partner in her urban subjects which are naturally founded on the complex relationships of the urban citizen and urban politics.

Invigorated by Spring
Oil on canvas. 30" x 48"
2016

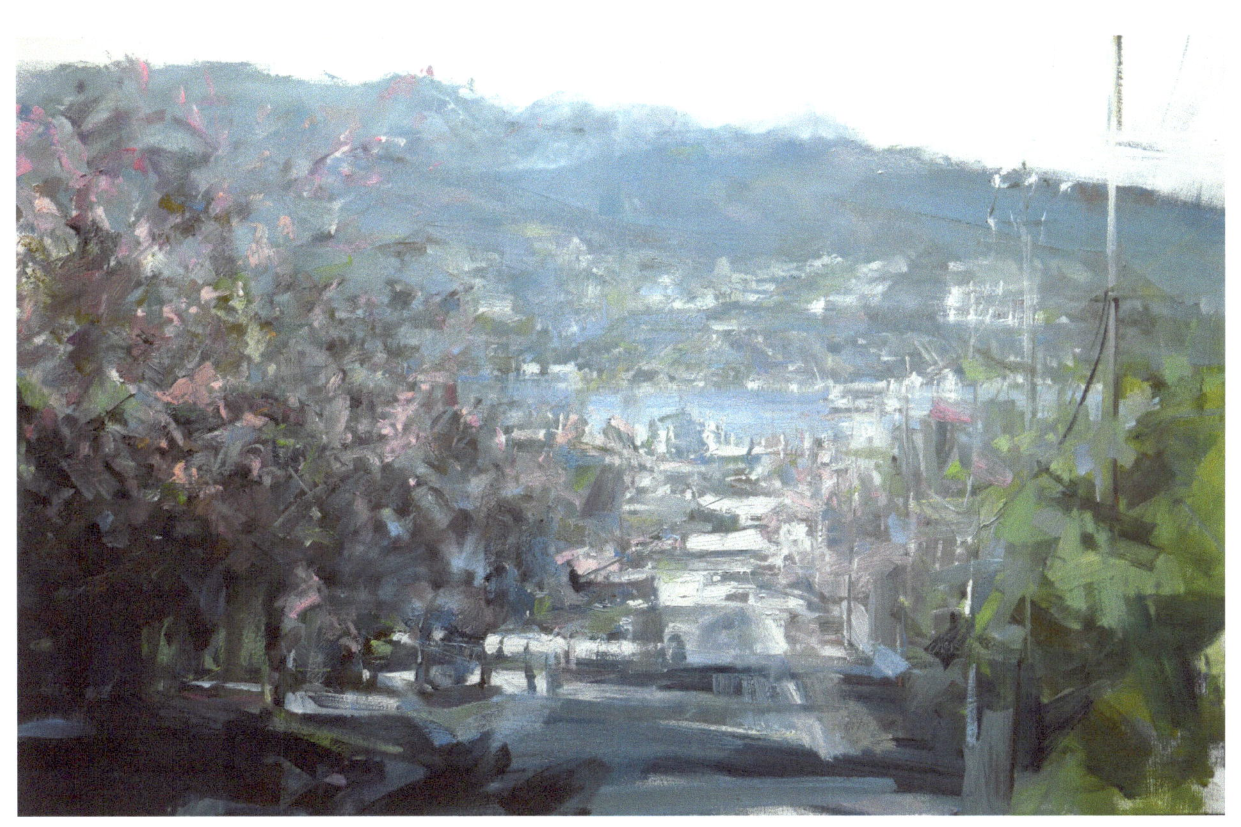

Tumbling through the streets of Vancouver
Oil on canvas. 10" x 10"
2018

I was regretting not having read the full article on Houdini and clearly stopping my own breath to synchronize my heart with hers, wasn't going to be effective.

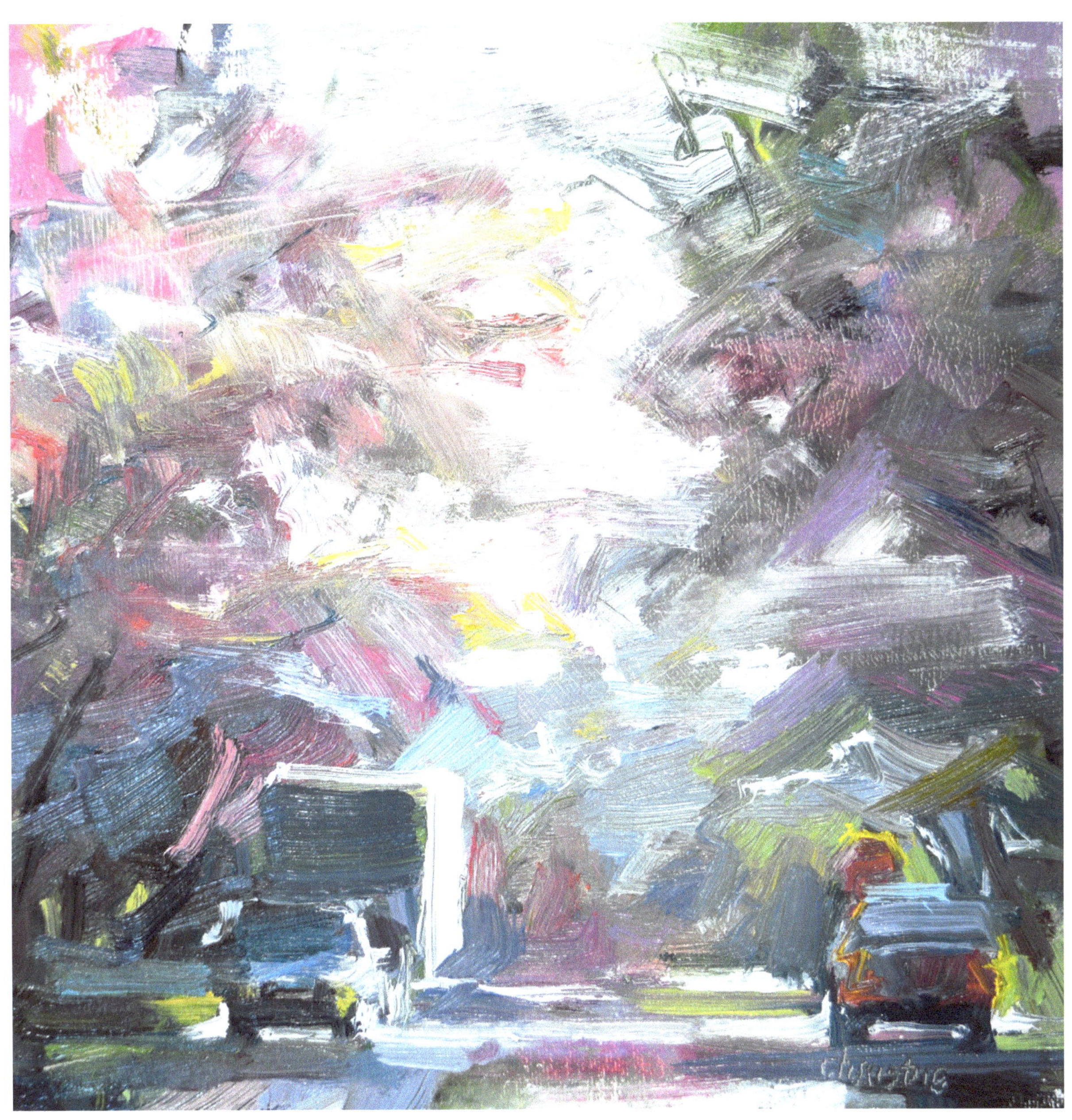
christine

Waterfront Parking
Oil on canvas. 10" x 10"
2015

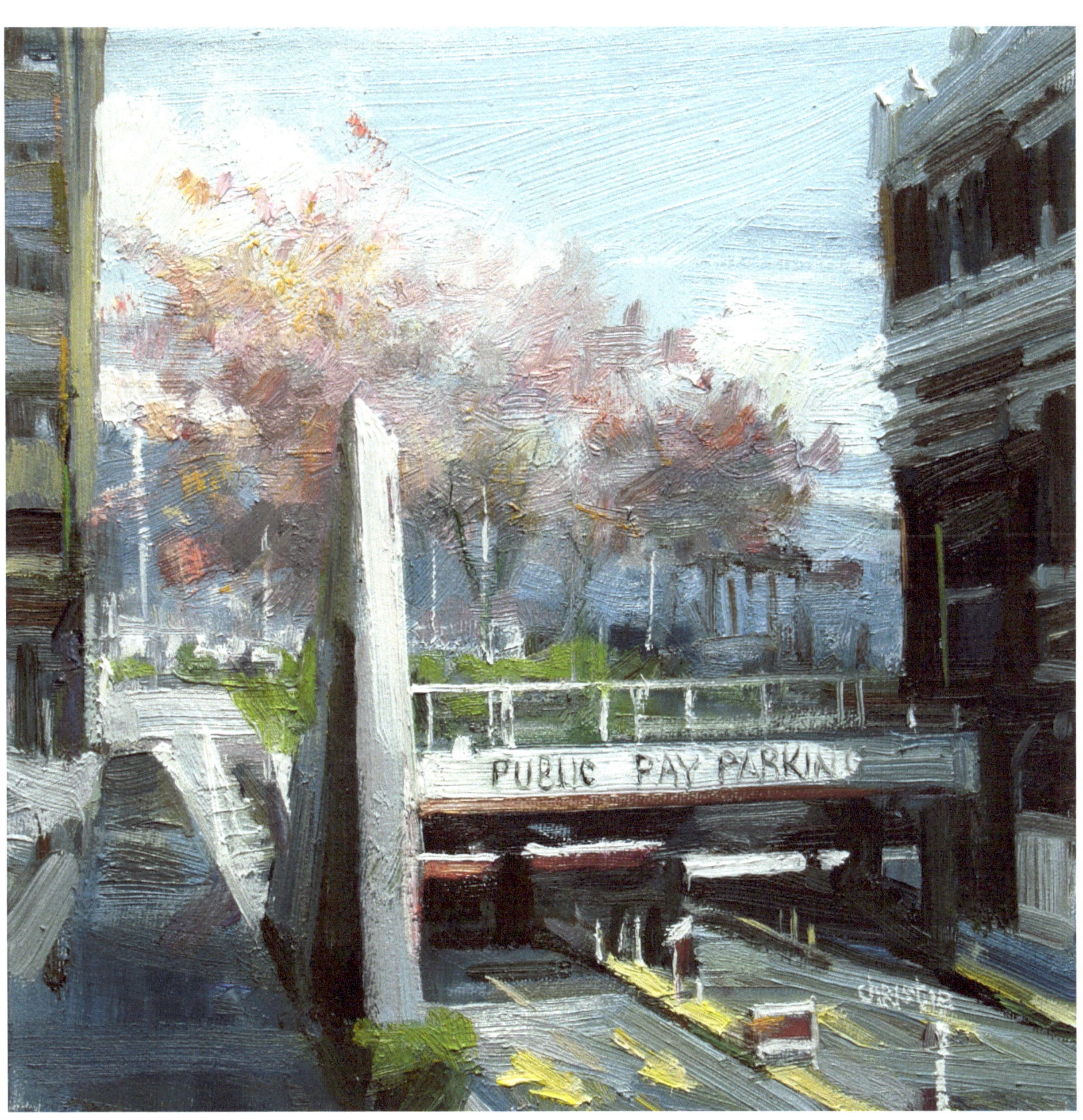
PUBLIC PAY PARKING

April in Vancouver

Oil on canvas. 10" x 10"

2014

The priest droned through his 30-something minute sermon, a hypnotic soundtrack to my now more focused meditations in the dark, cool church. The life-size marble statues along the aisles protected us not from our mortal shame but the hot South African Saturday evening.

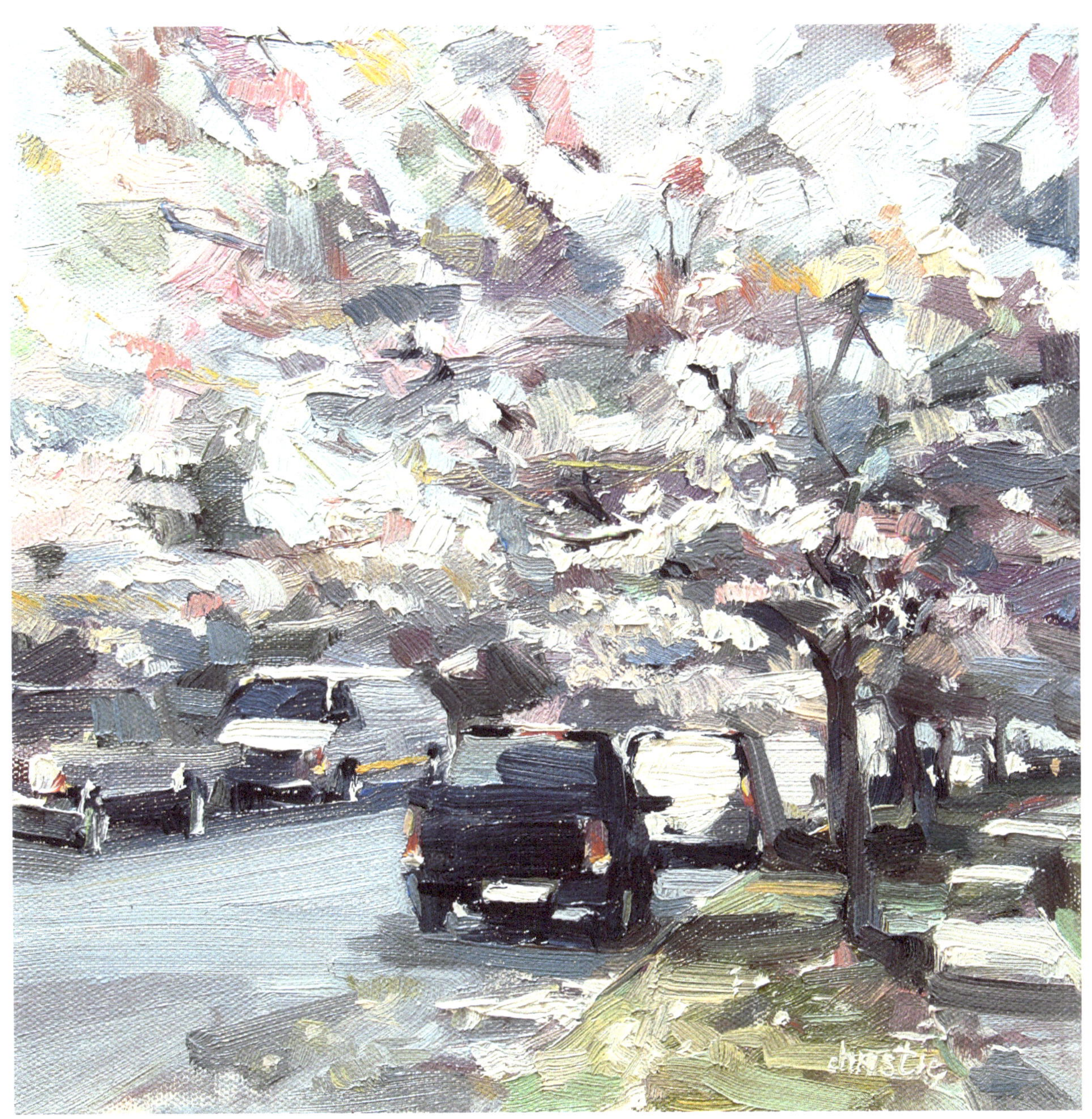
christie

Burrard Blossom

Oil on canvas. 10" x 10"

2015

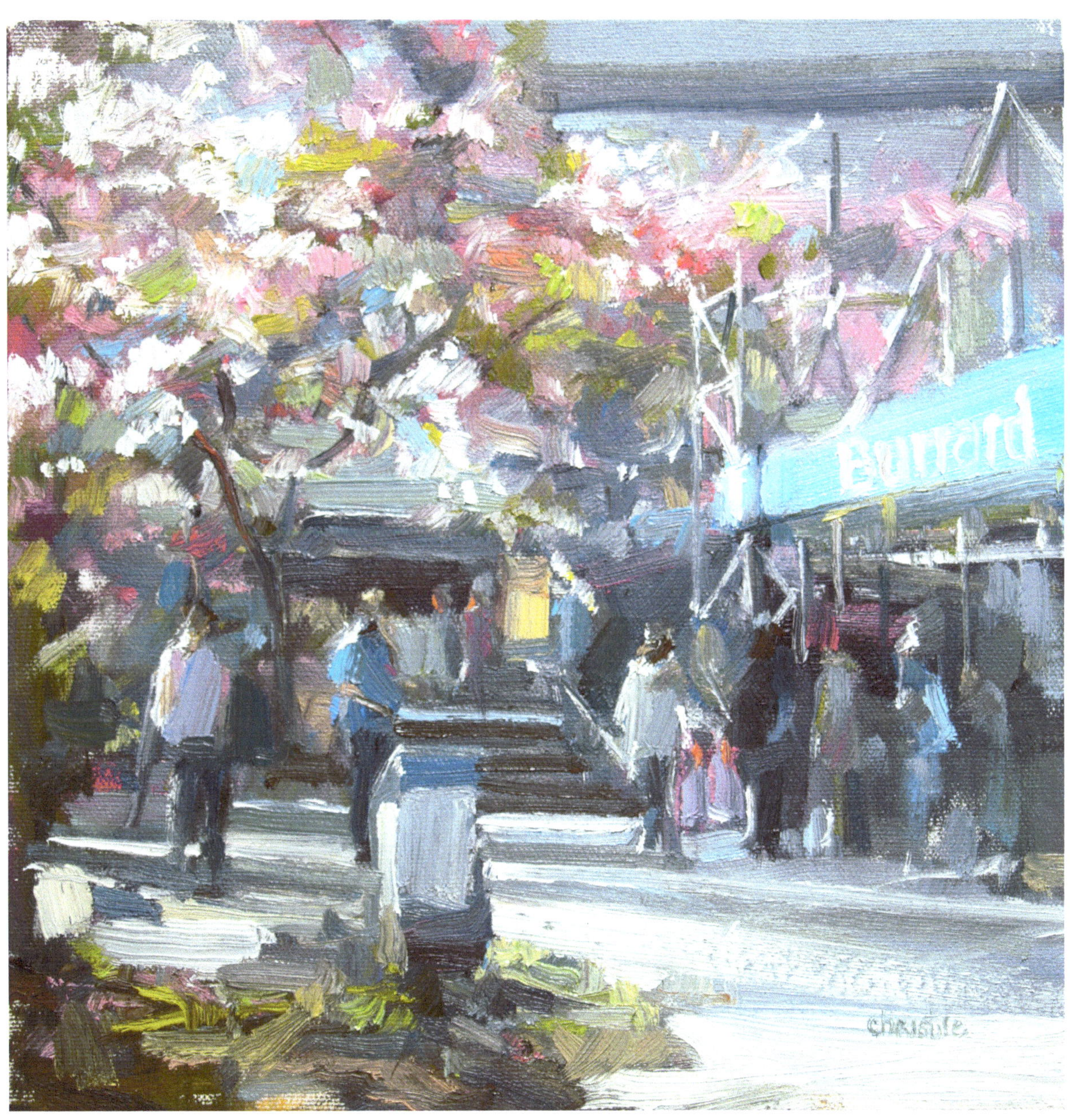
Burrard
christie

Diving Deeper

Oil on canvas. 10" x 10"

2018

It is clear logic, I thought as I rested my head against my grandmother's soft, rhythmic bosom, once our hearts were trained to beat at the same time when hers stopped so would mine.

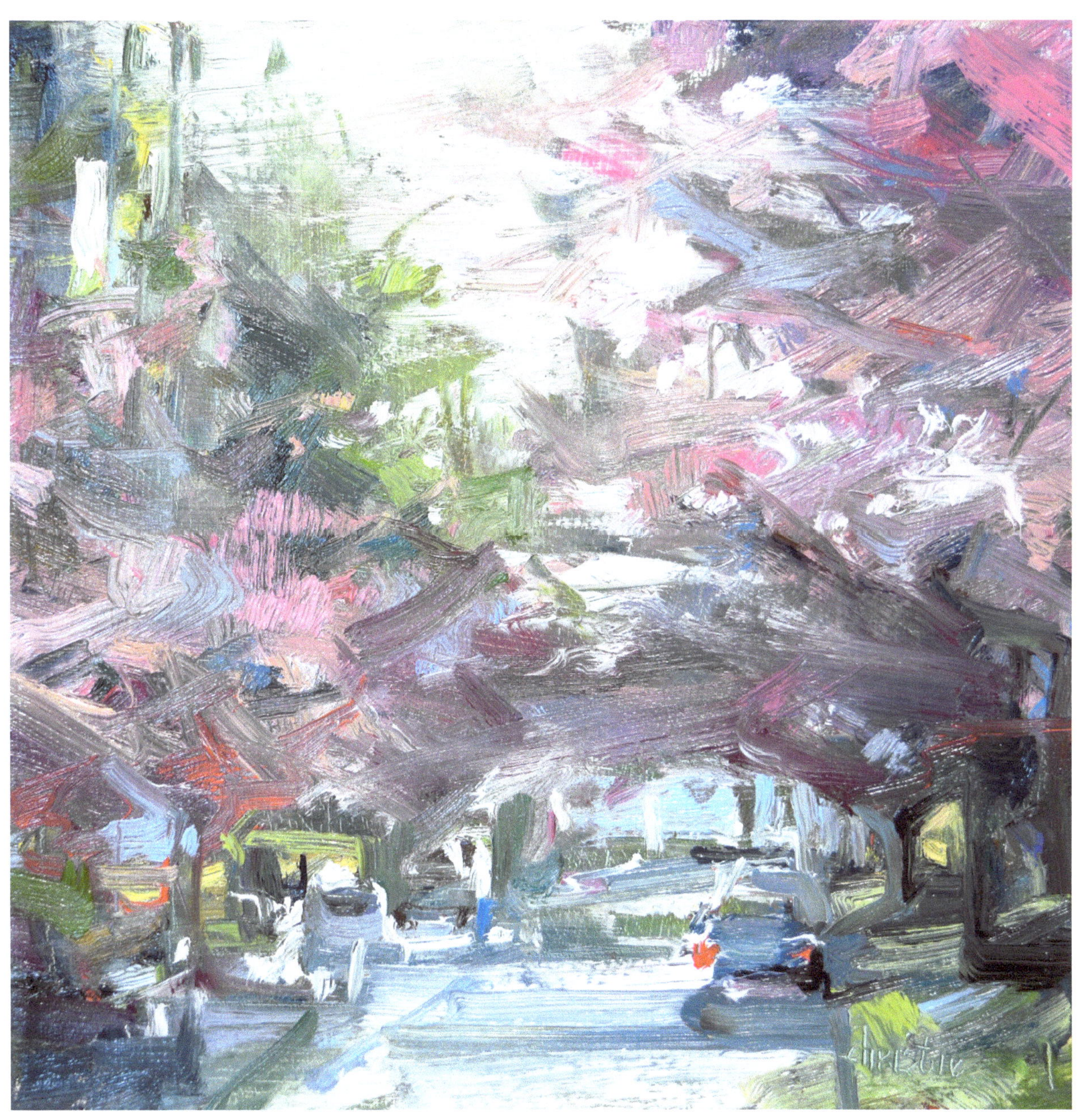

Beechwood

Oil on canvas. 10" x 10"

2014

She was my love grandmother, my maternal grandmother, with a soft warm body that a small girl could always find a spot to cuddle into. She was also the other side of the simmering war in our house that was grounded in people I had never met and in spaces that I had never visited.

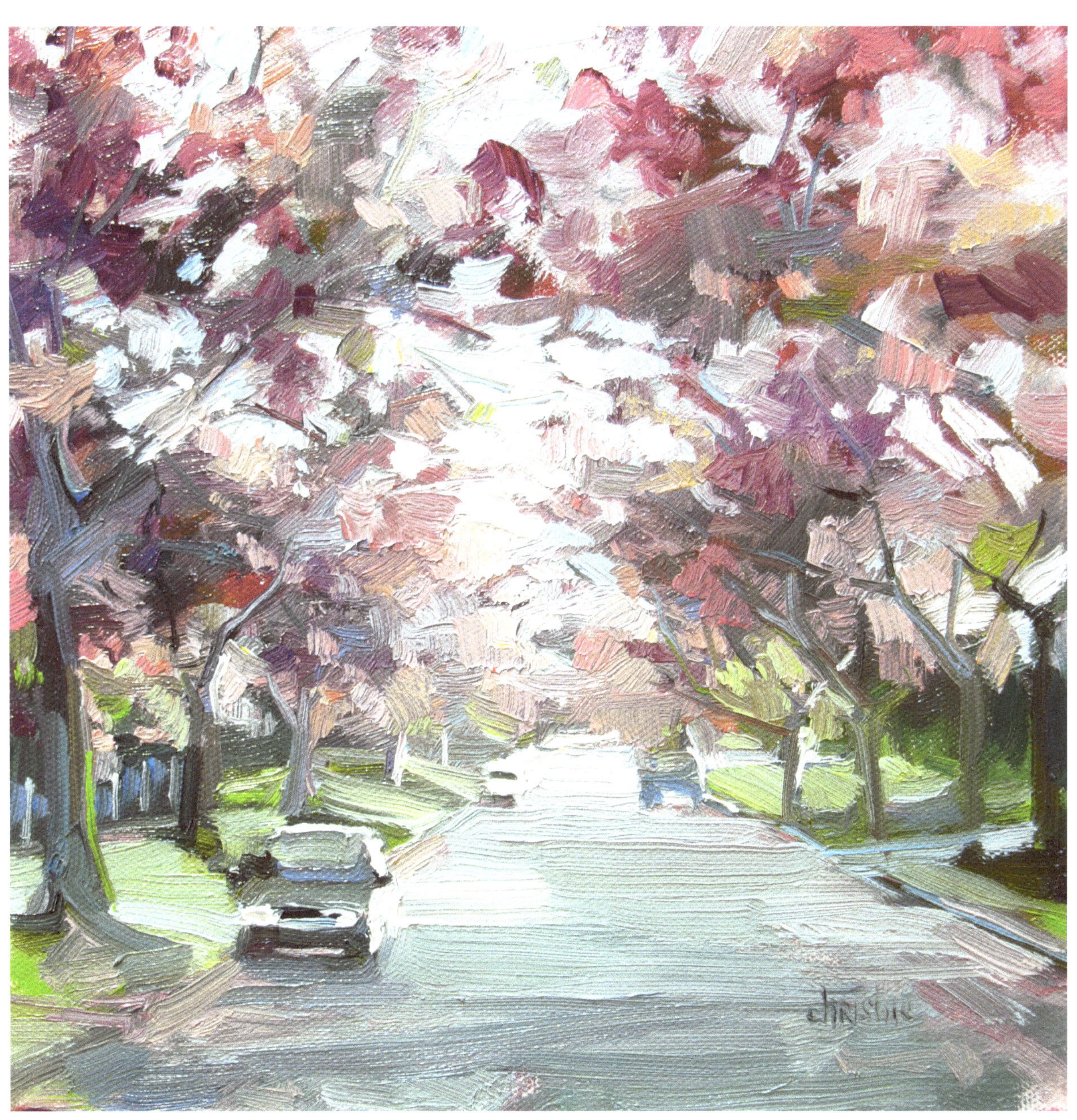

Downtown Spring
Oil on canvas. 10" x 10"
2014

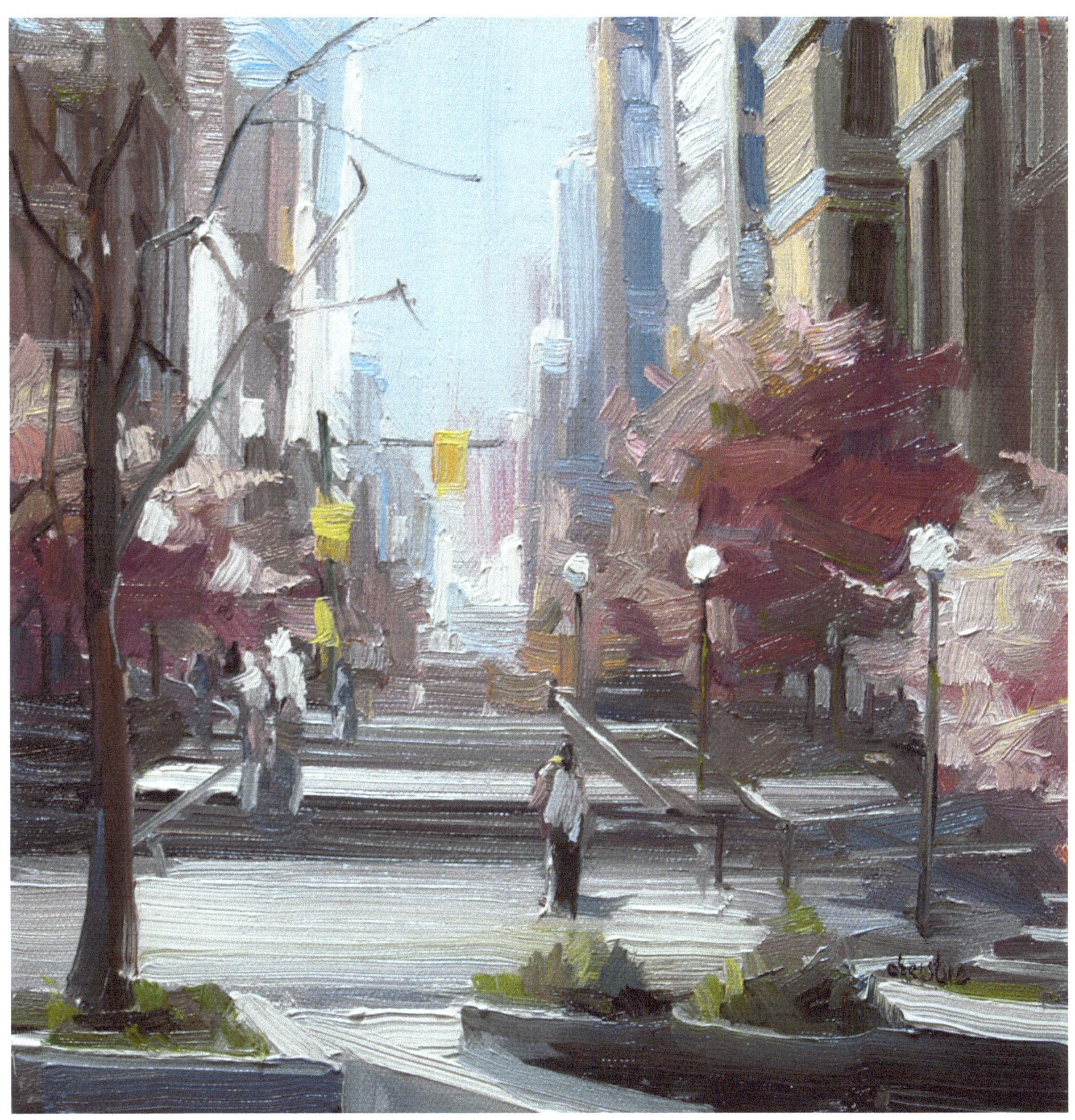

School Days.

Oil on canvas. 10" x 10"

2014

Like suminagashi , in the vague days of memory I had met my paternal grandfather. I understood him by his ripples on his son and wife who suddenly found herself widowed from a 1940's marriage, as she approach her 50's.

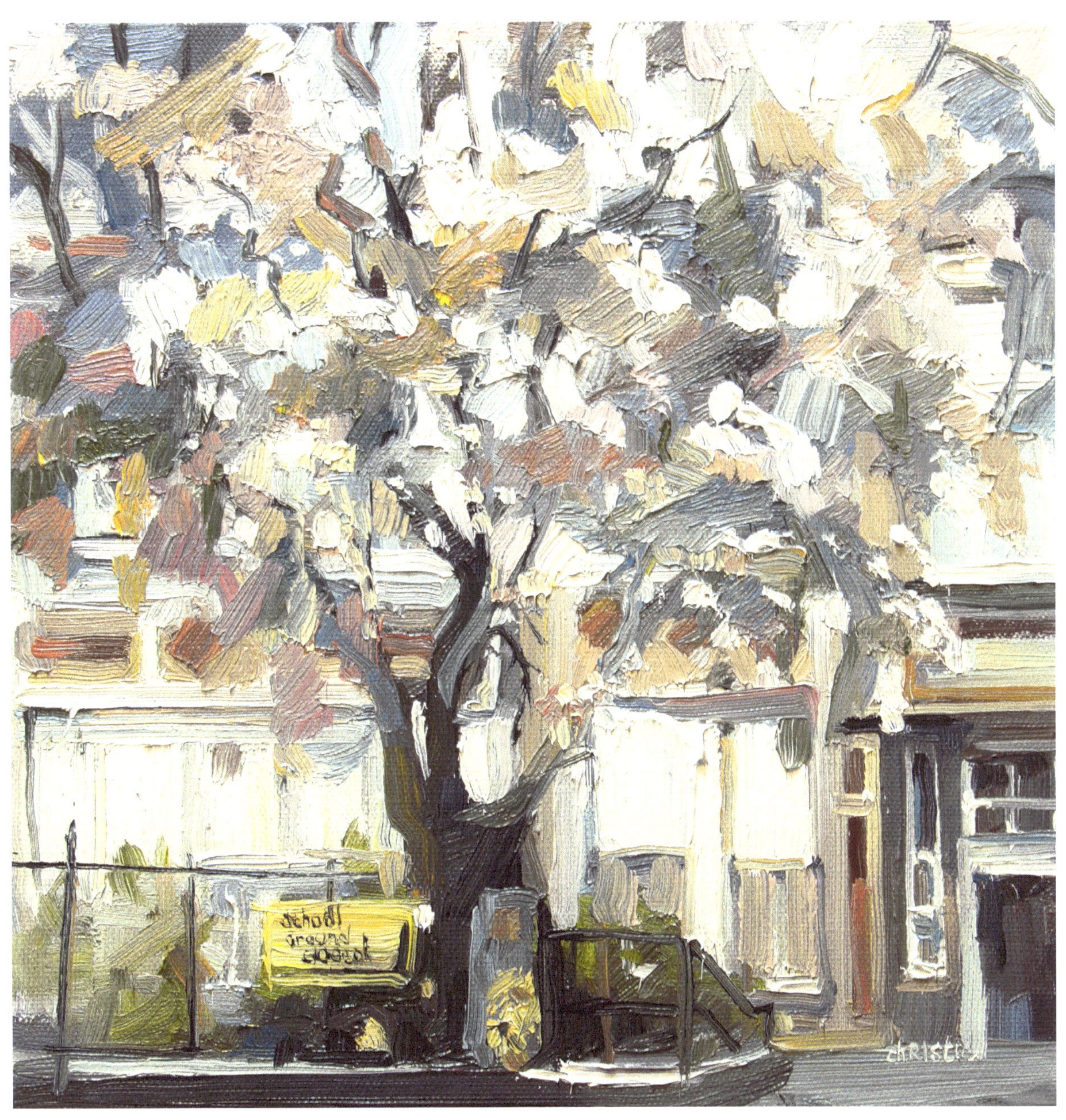

Spring Settles Slowly
Oil on canvas. 10" x 10"
2016

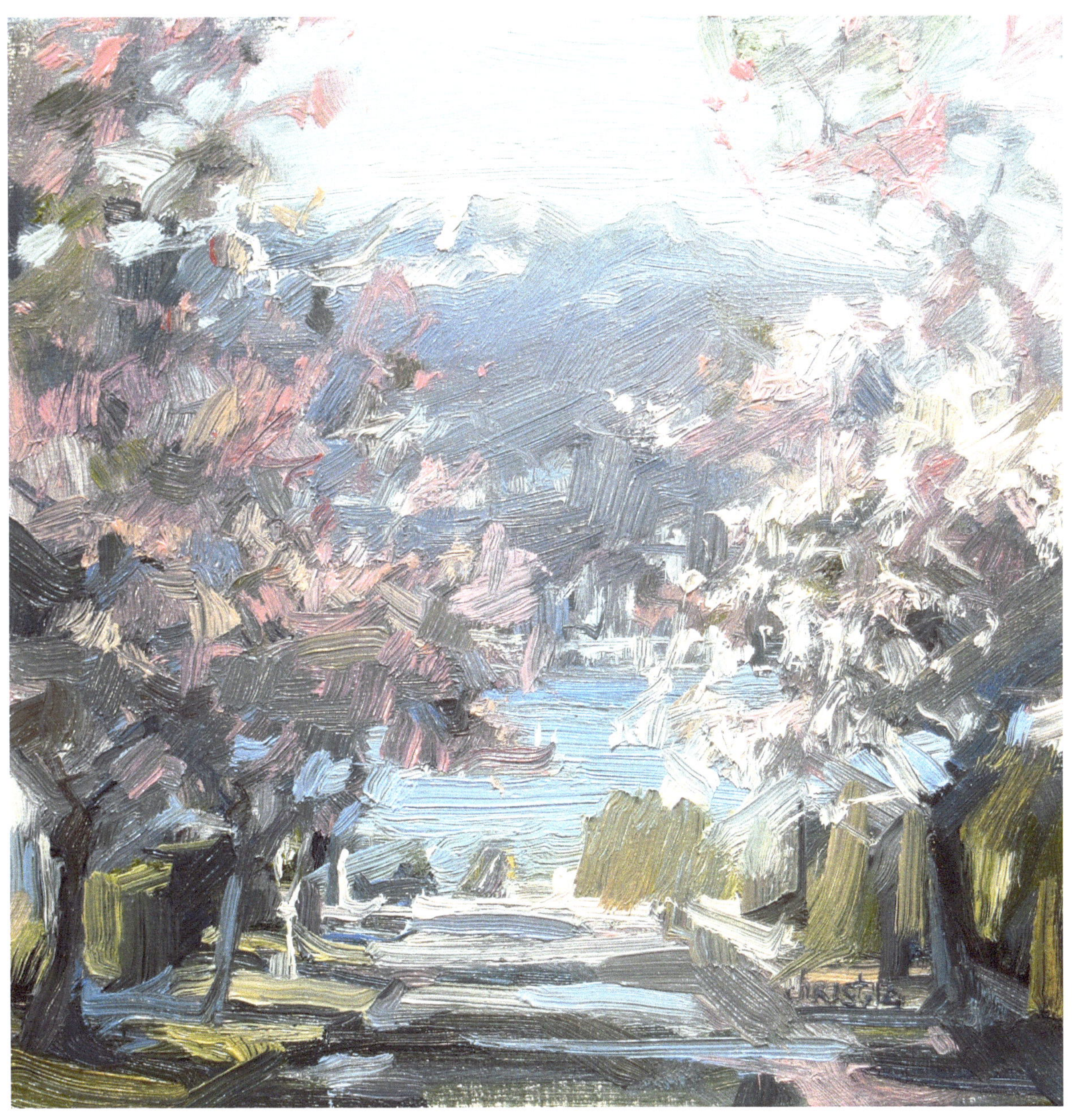

The Regent of Burrard
Oil on canvas. 10" x 10"
2015

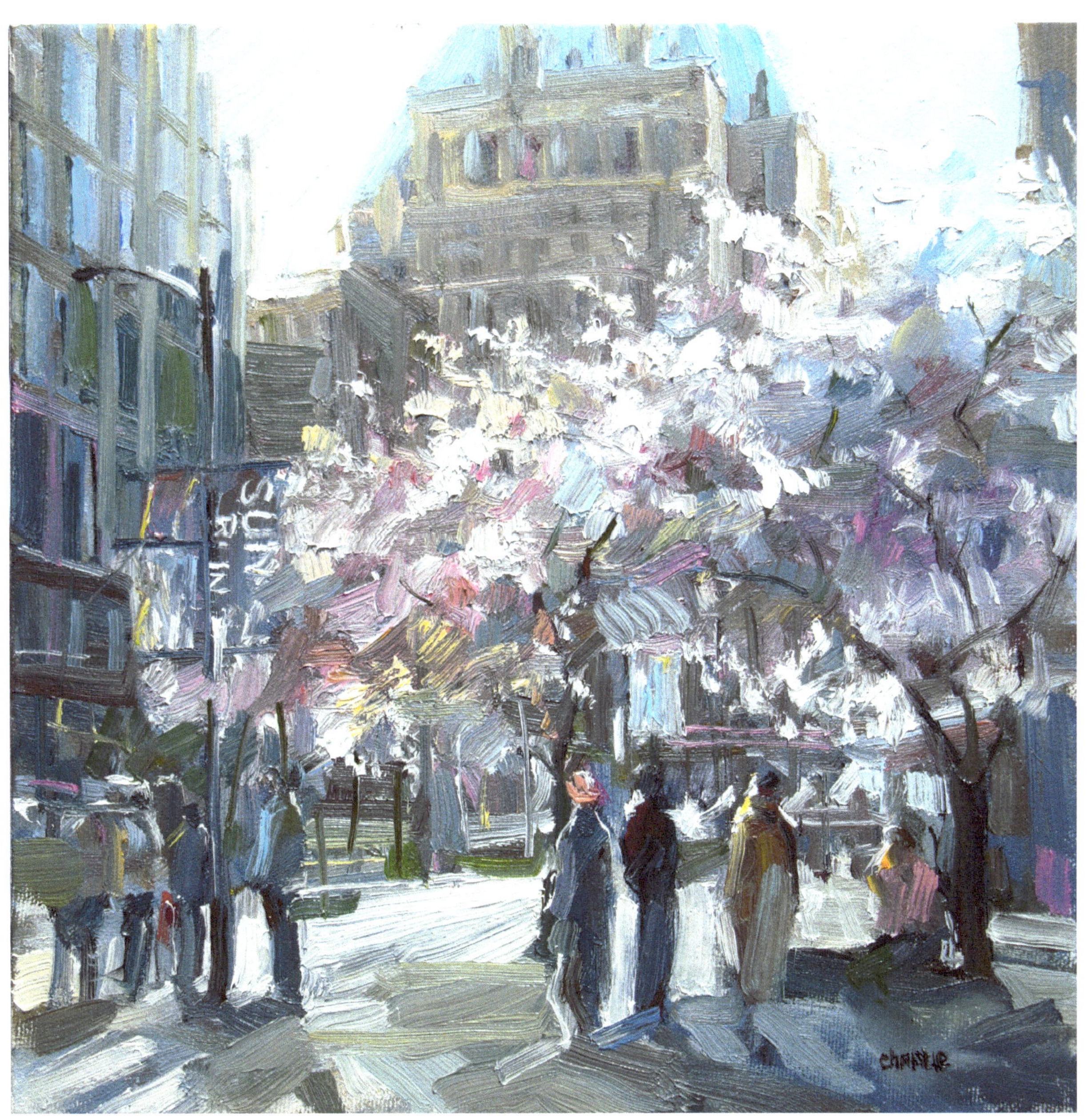

Playing Beneath the Blossoms

Oil on canvas. 10" x 10"

2015

The women of my family were the most exciting, unpredictable and invigorating. They were the strongest, in possession of a quiet dominance and my paternal grandmother stood the tallest. In widowhood, she was determined, independent, alive and resilient.

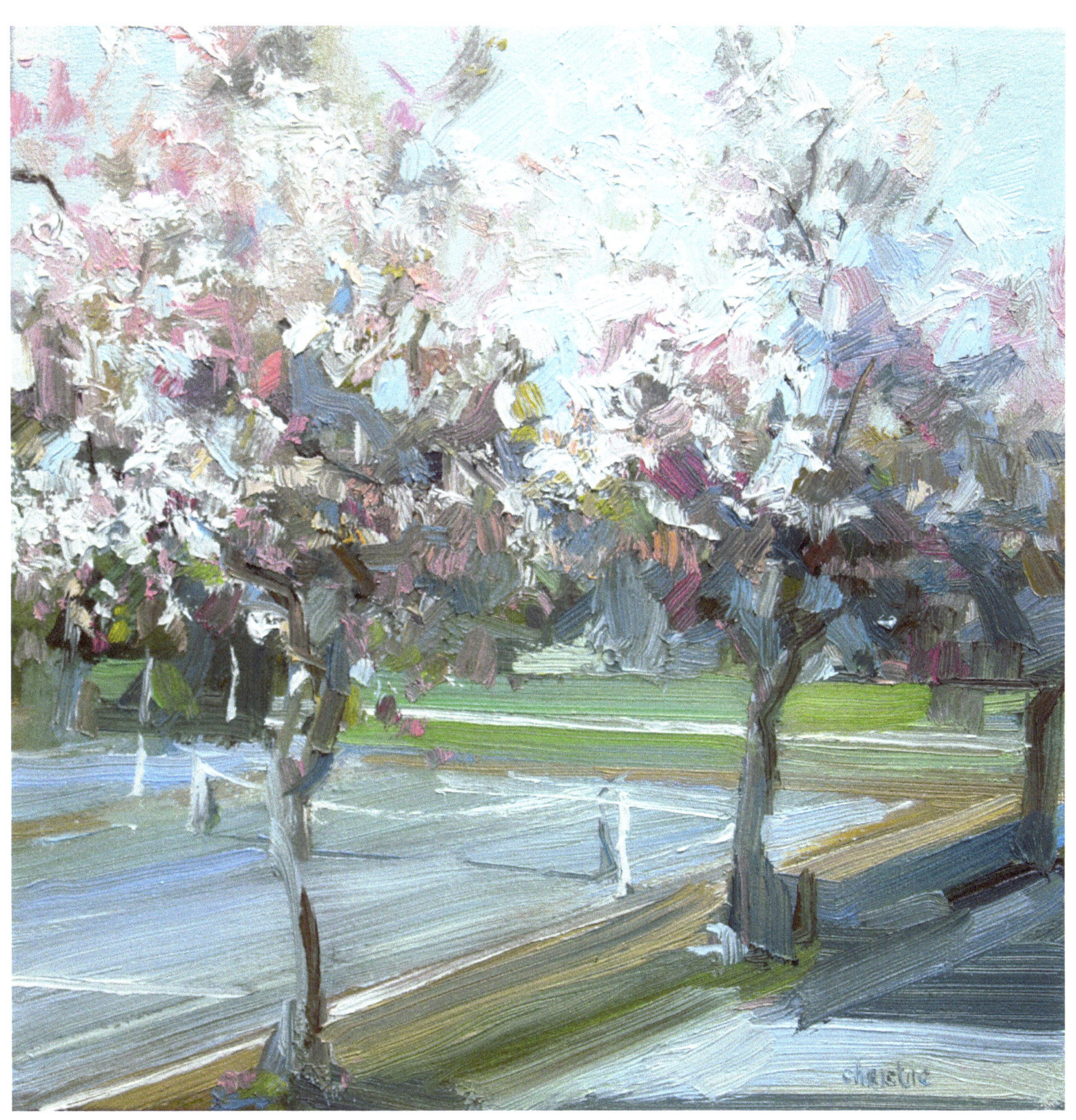

Beechwood Ave on an April Morning

Oil on canvas. 10" x 10"

2014

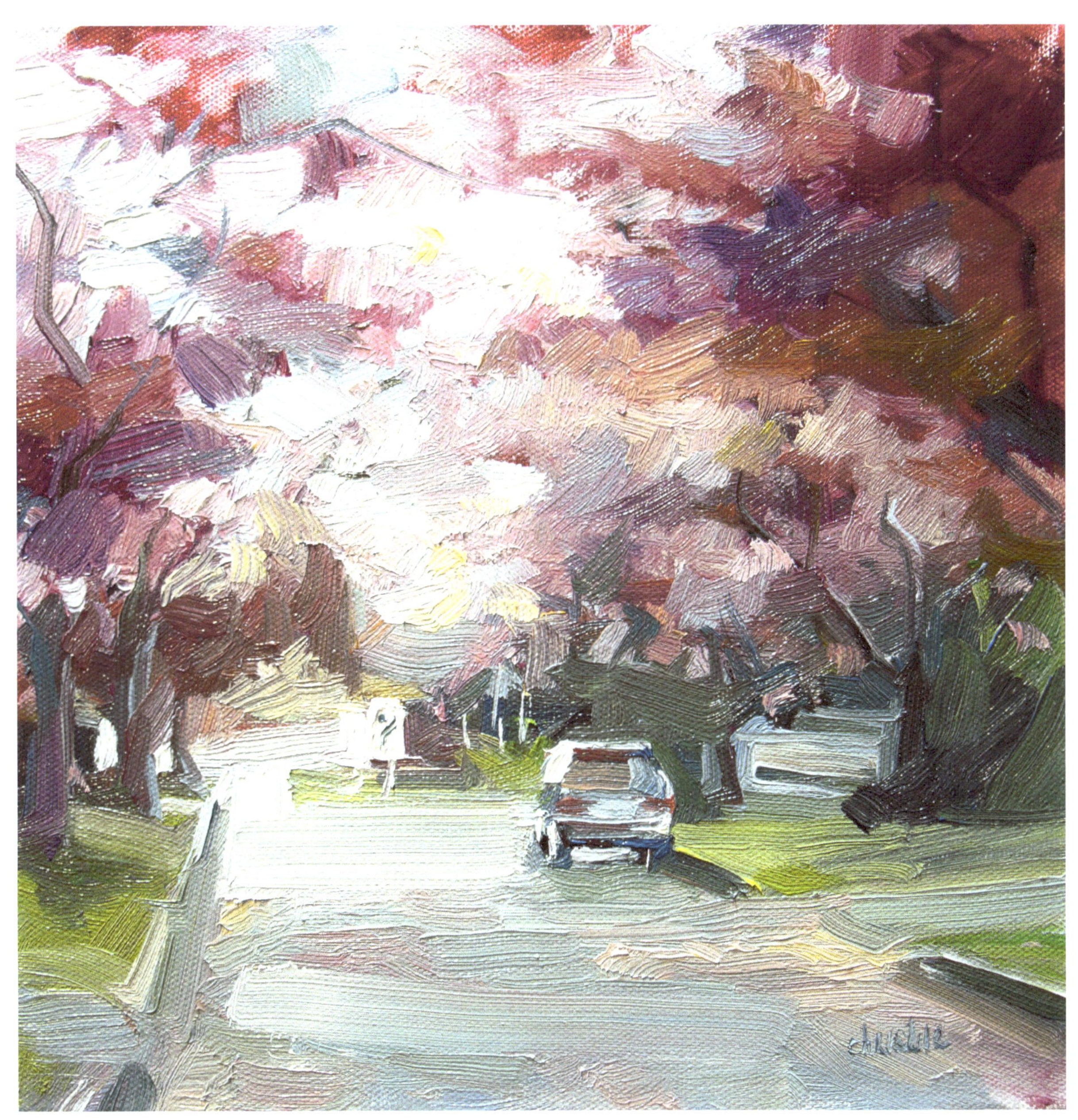

Coal Harbour Cascade

Oil on canvas. 10" x 10"

2015

“Shotgun!” was a word below my mother's privilege and as usual I sat alongside my sisters, behind my father with my head cautiously resting on the edge of the mechanically rolled down window.

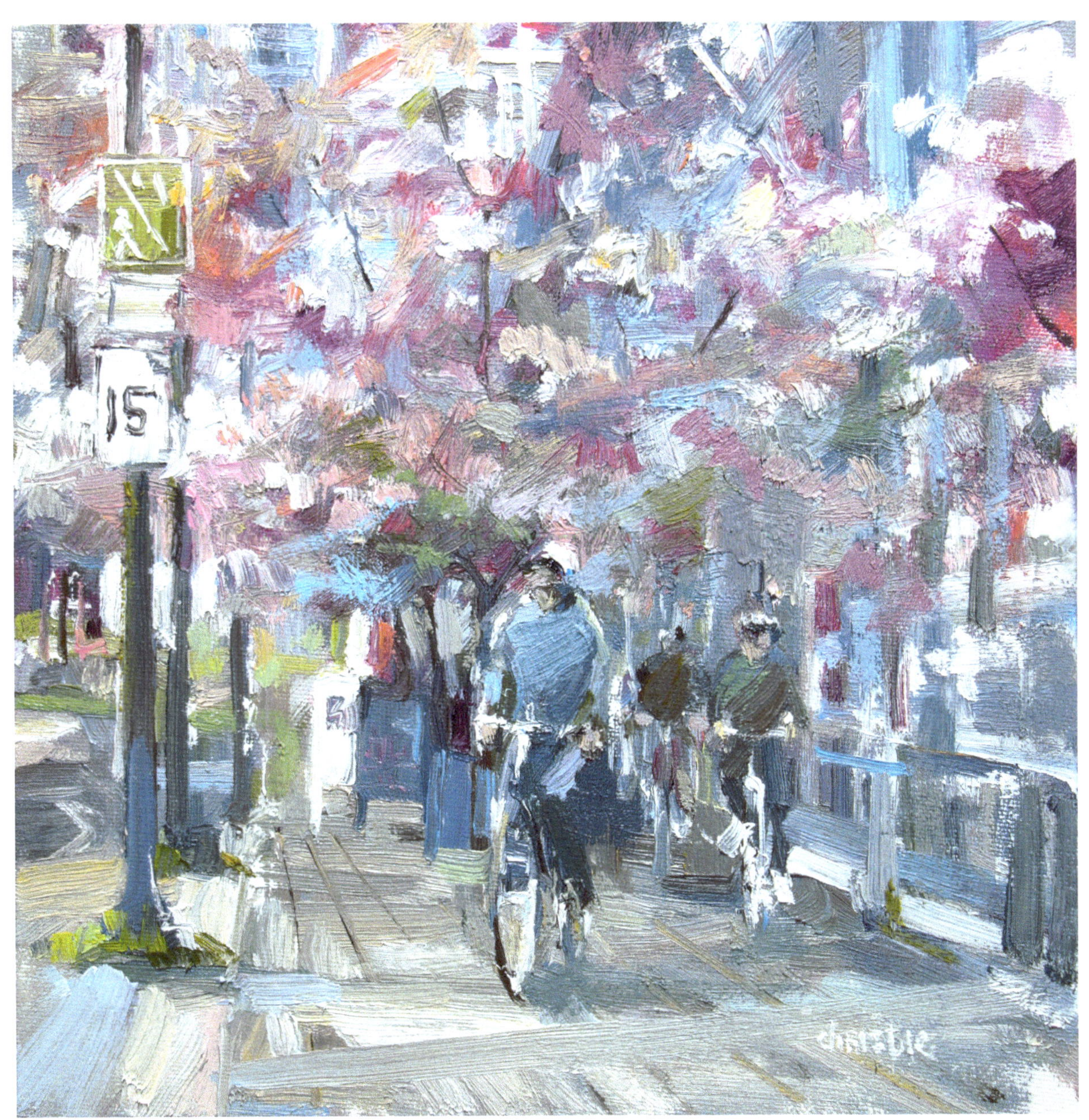
15

North of Gore

Oil on canvas. 10" x 10"

2018

It wasn't that I was observant of his admonition that things fleshy and protruding from the car were to be summarily removed by unexpected passing objects. No, my young dog desires were restrained by the memory of the vicious head slap that I had received as our train slid from the platform and the gentle reminder through the shock of so much vengeance from a stranger, that this was inevitable when 2 soft stationary objects intersected at a slow pace.

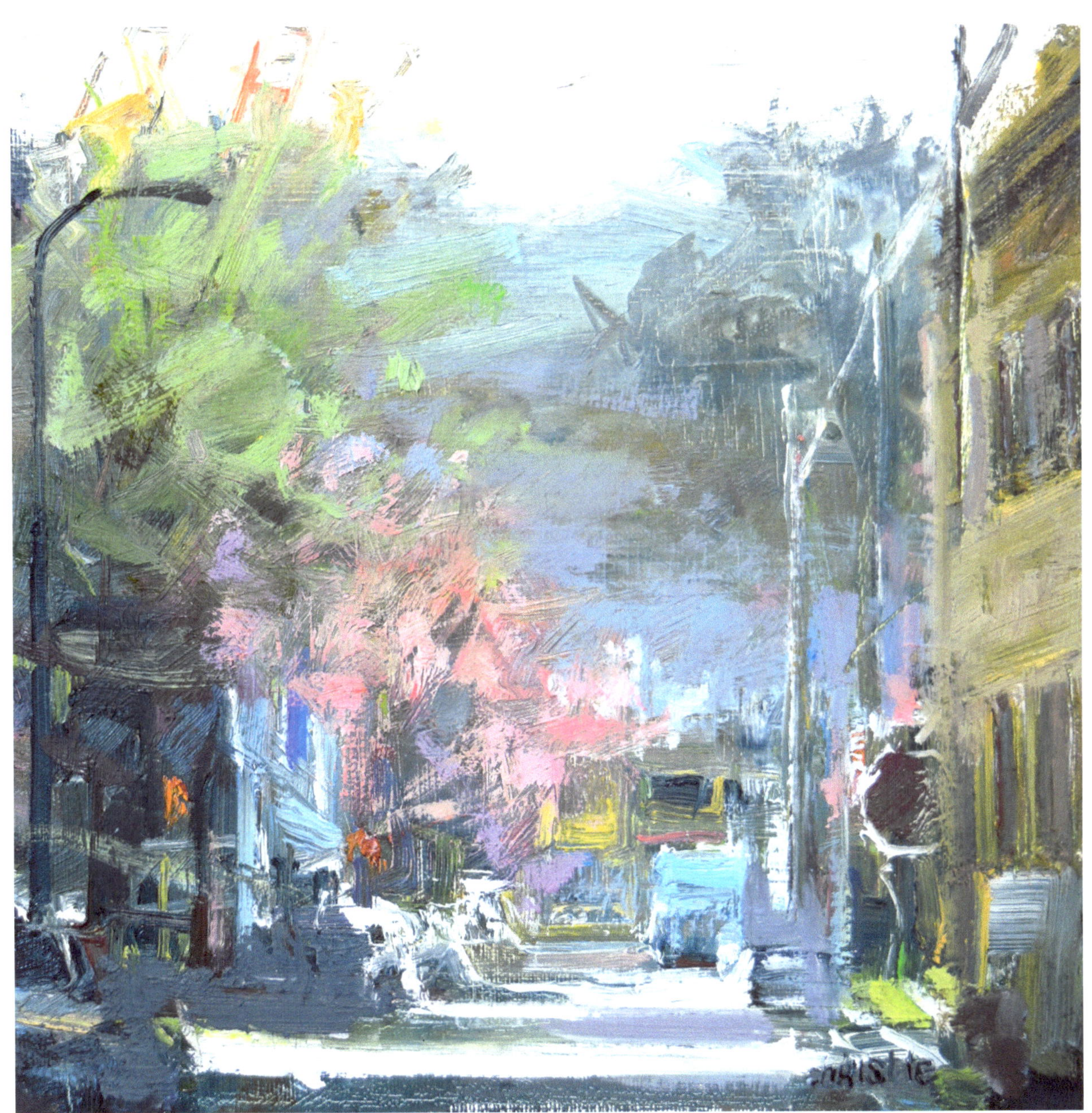

Cherry Blossom Crescendo
Oil on canvas. 10" x 10"
2015

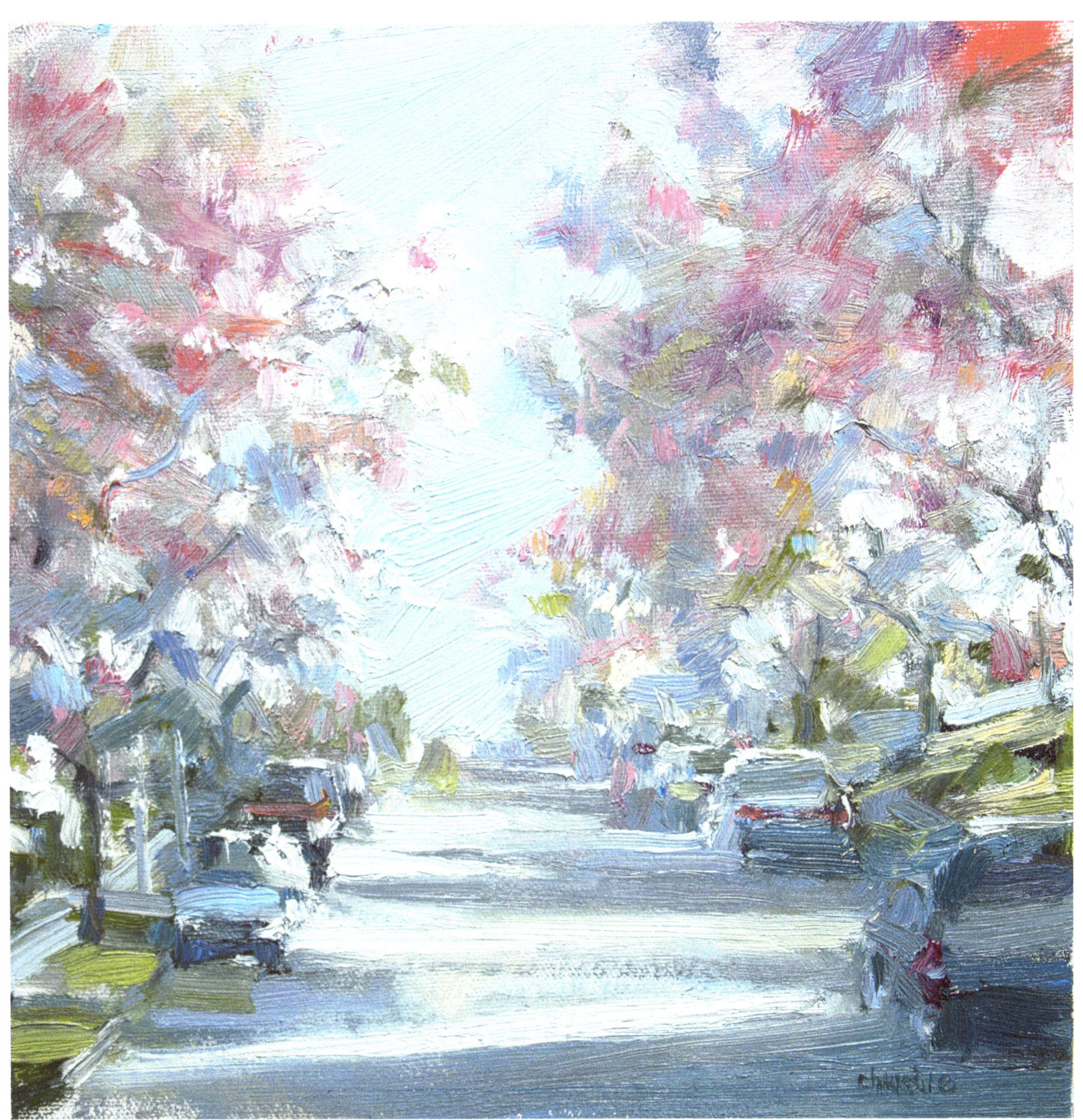

Just off Yew

Oil on canvas. 10" x 10"

2013

The anticipated pleasure that hearing the loud chattering voices of the women would bring, balanced the scales of danger. I would know that they were standing in the kitchen, their hands as busy as their words.

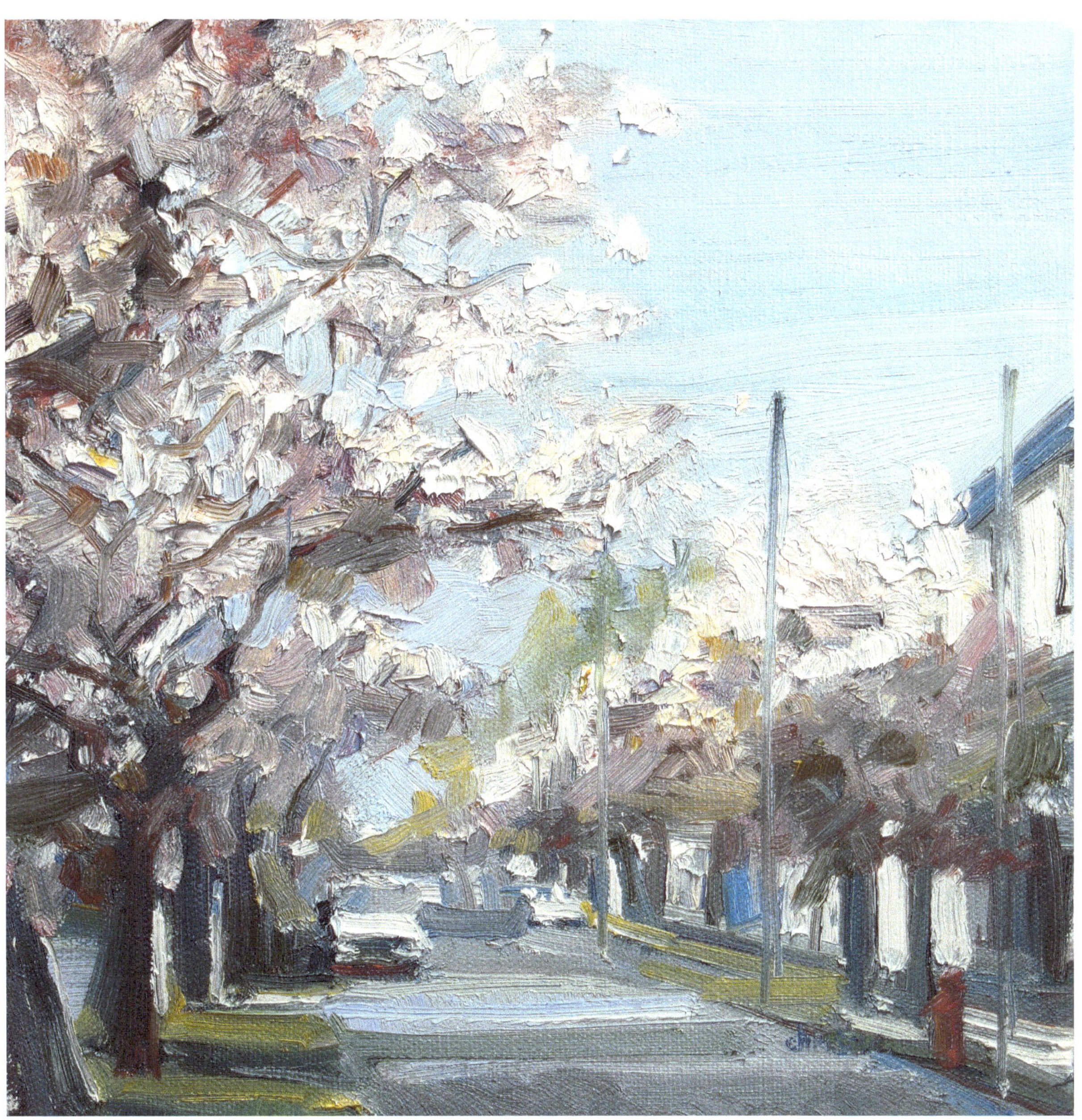

The Corner Detour

Oil on canvas. 10" x 10"

2018

We trawled my grandmother's complex searching for a legitimate open car space and the warm weekend air carried the smell of jasmine dancing on top of my grandmother's voice that reverberated through the iron railings that lined the walkways of the flats. Not louder, only more alive and colourful.

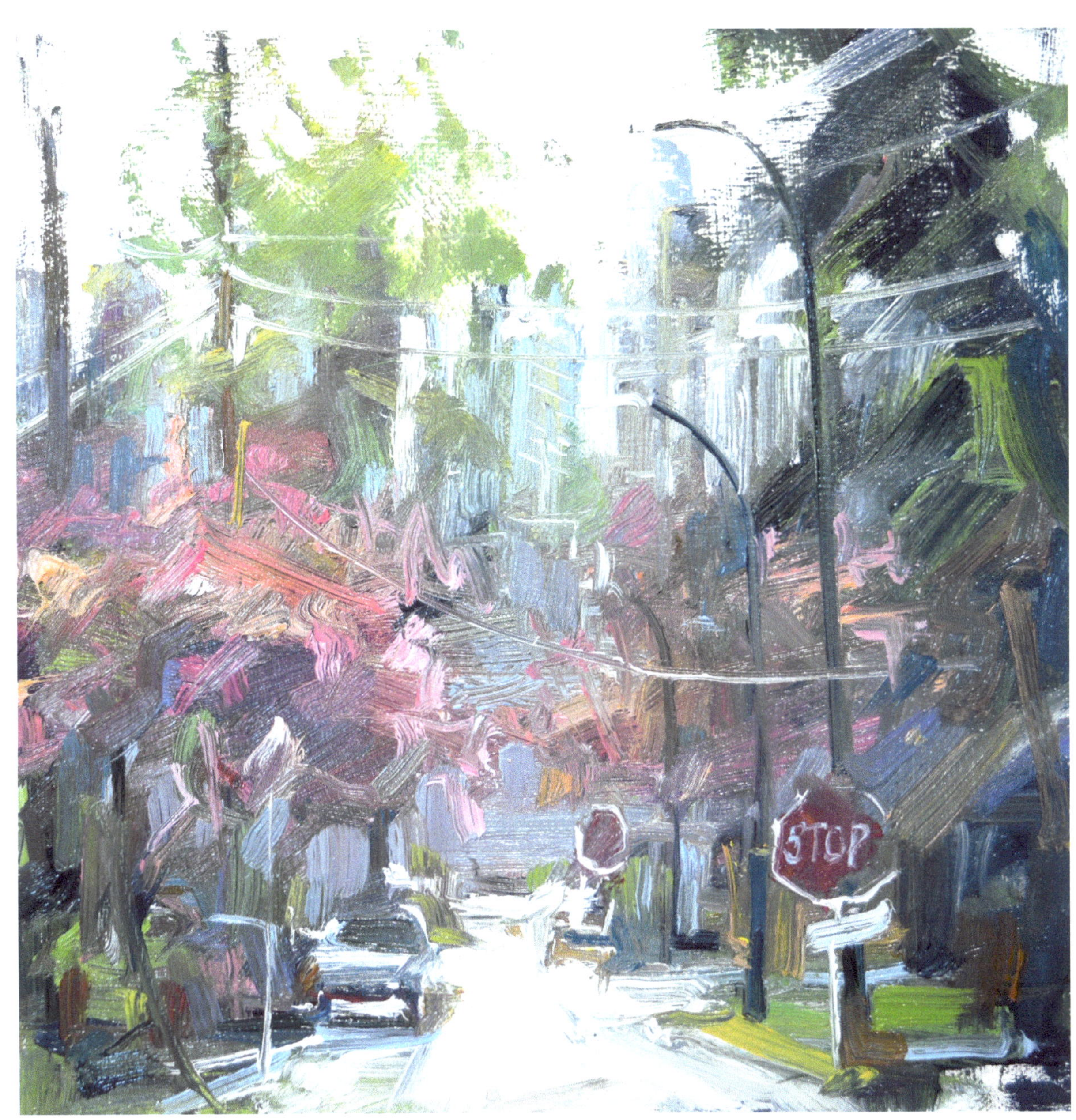
STOP

Burnaby Spring
Oil on canvas. 10" x 10"
2014

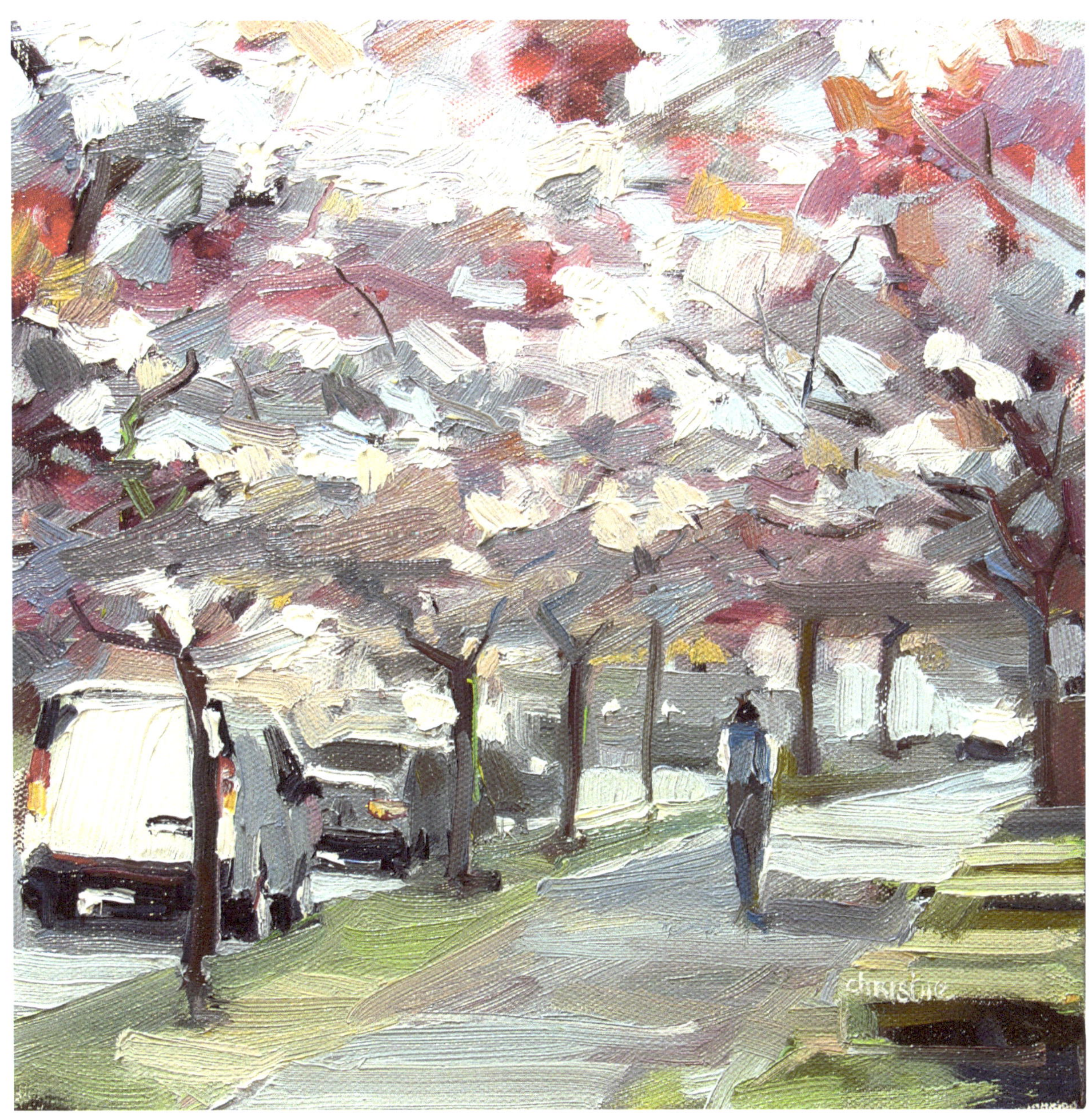
christine

Cherry Blossoms
Oil on canvas. 10" x 10"
2014

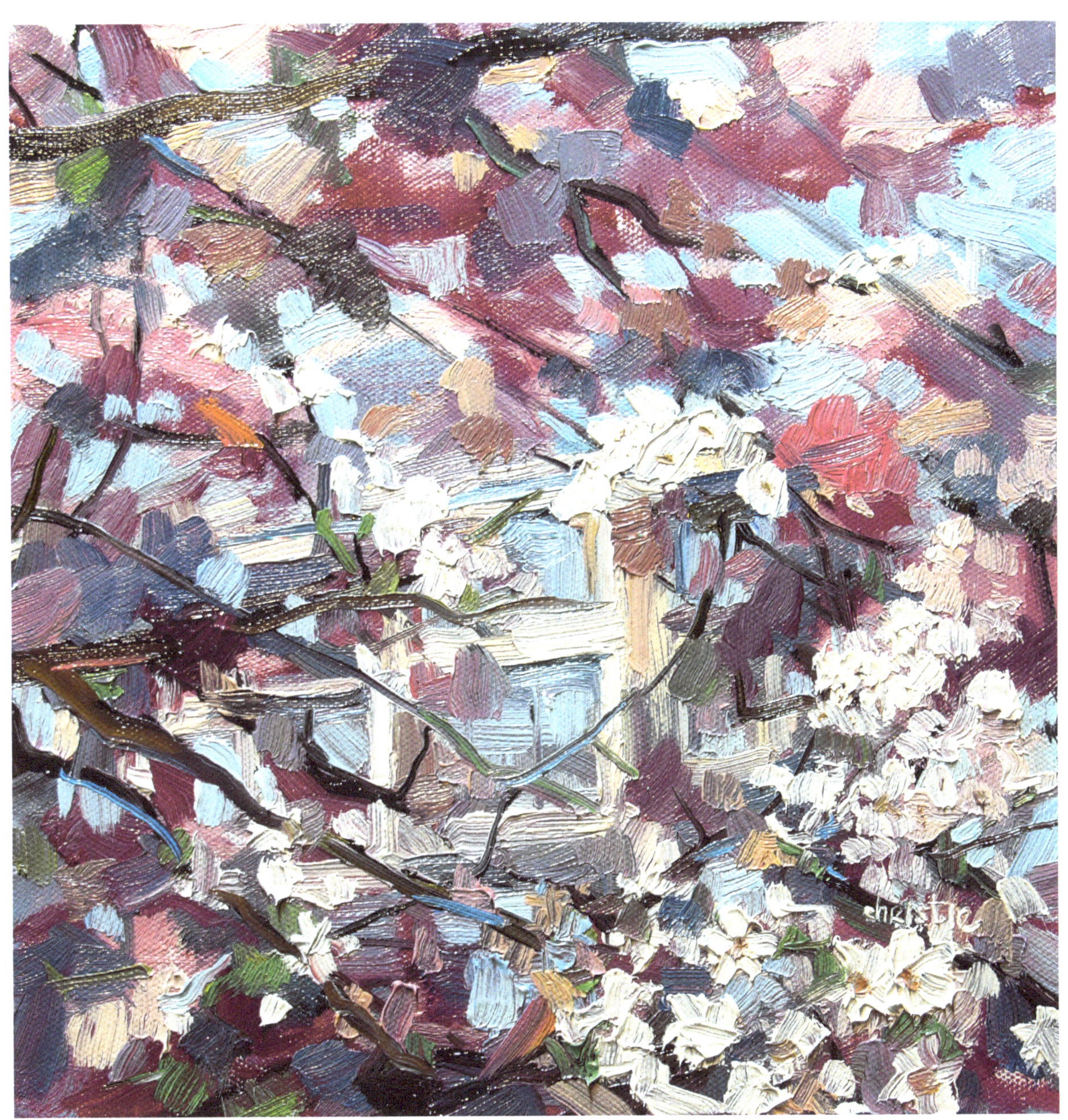
christie

Blossoming Memories

Oil on canvas. 10" x 10"

2015

My maternal grandmother shared her time between our home and that of my godfather's and it was during one of her periods away that she stopped coming back.

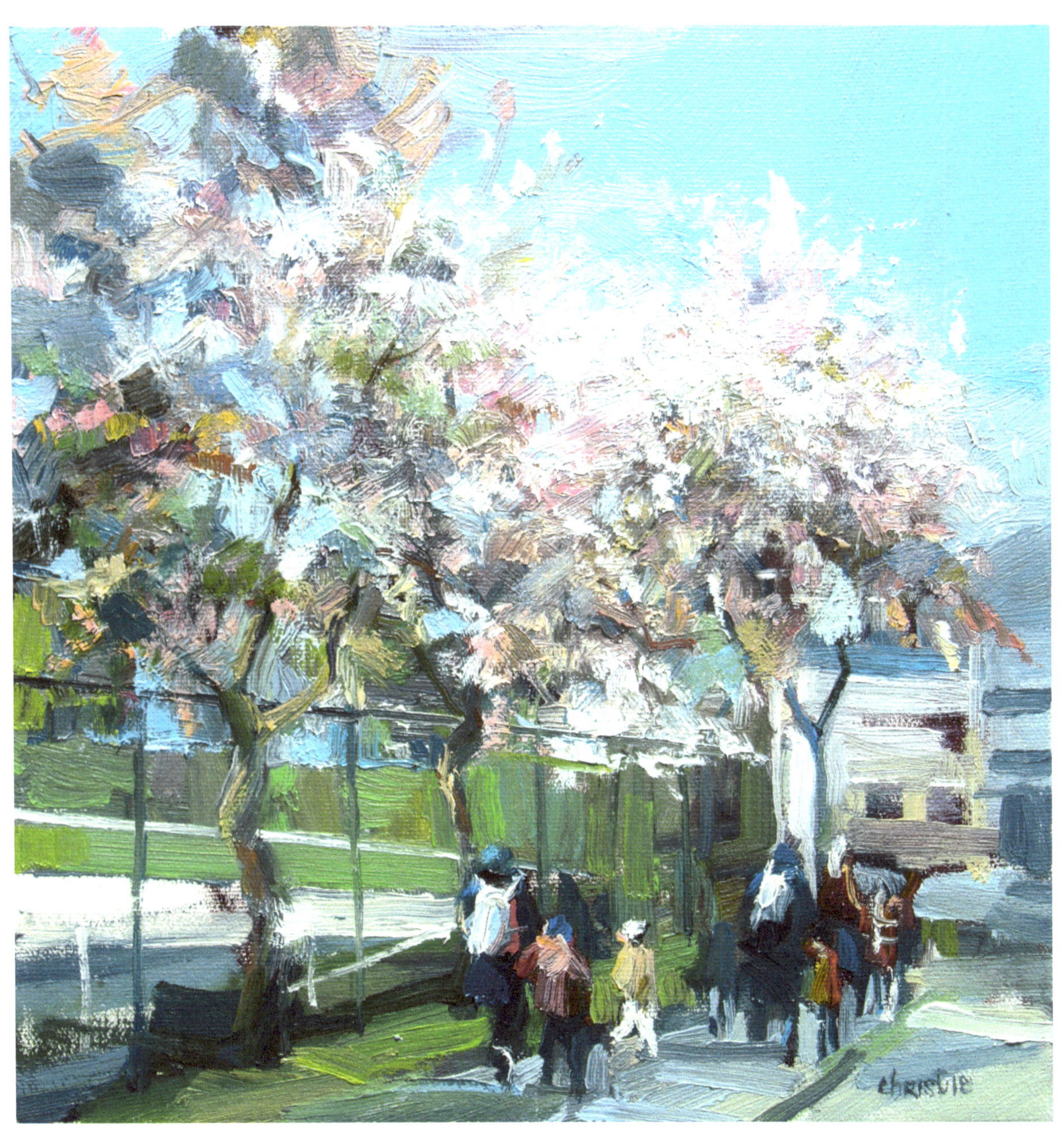
christie

Secret Springtime Streets
Oil on canvas. 10" x 10"
2015

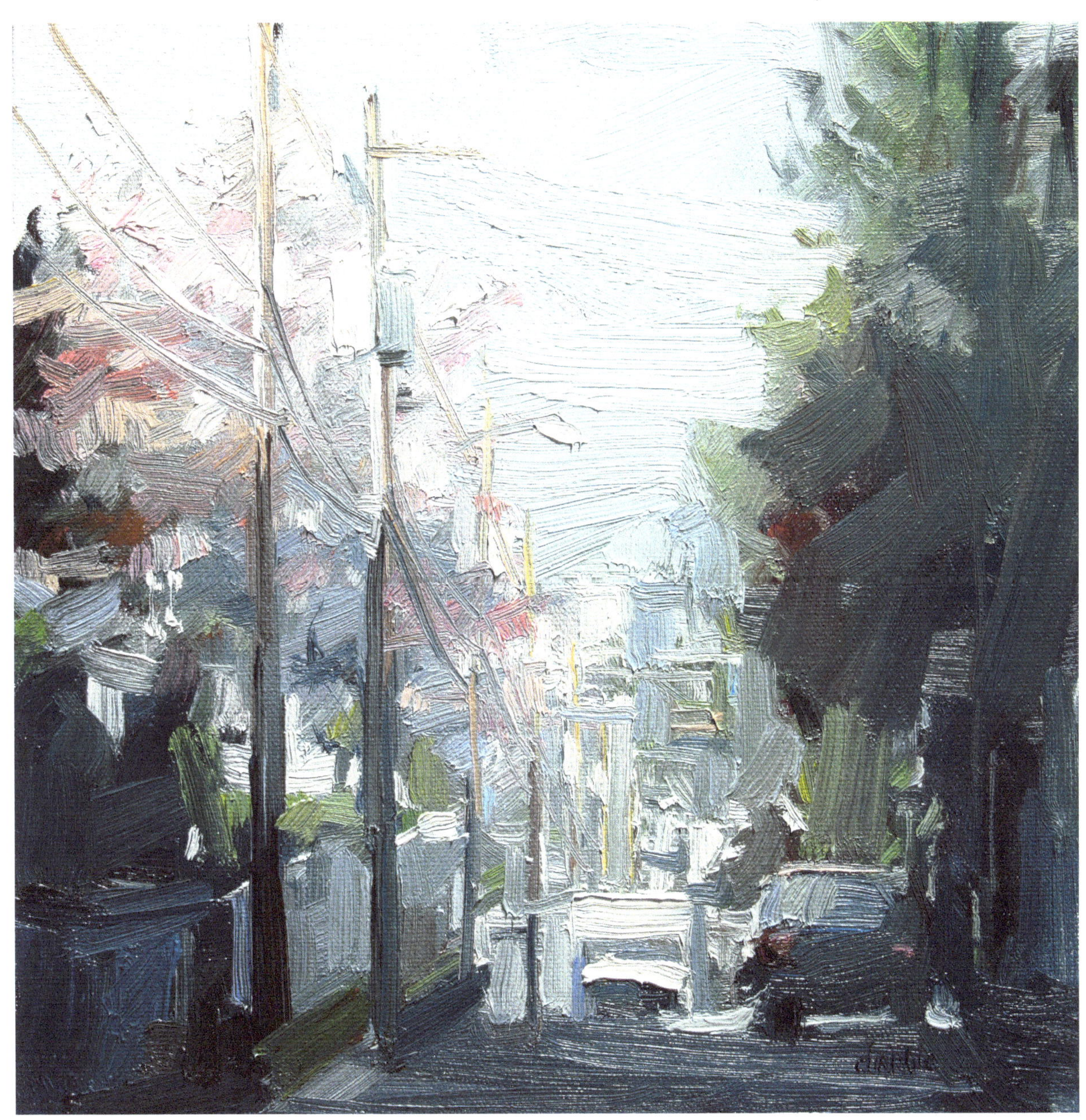

Tuesday Morning on Cornwall

Oil on canvas. 10" x 10"

2013

My paternal grandmother at 90 grows taller and even at opposite ends of the hemispheres, recently we made new memories but here's a thing - the thing. Memories are place-based.

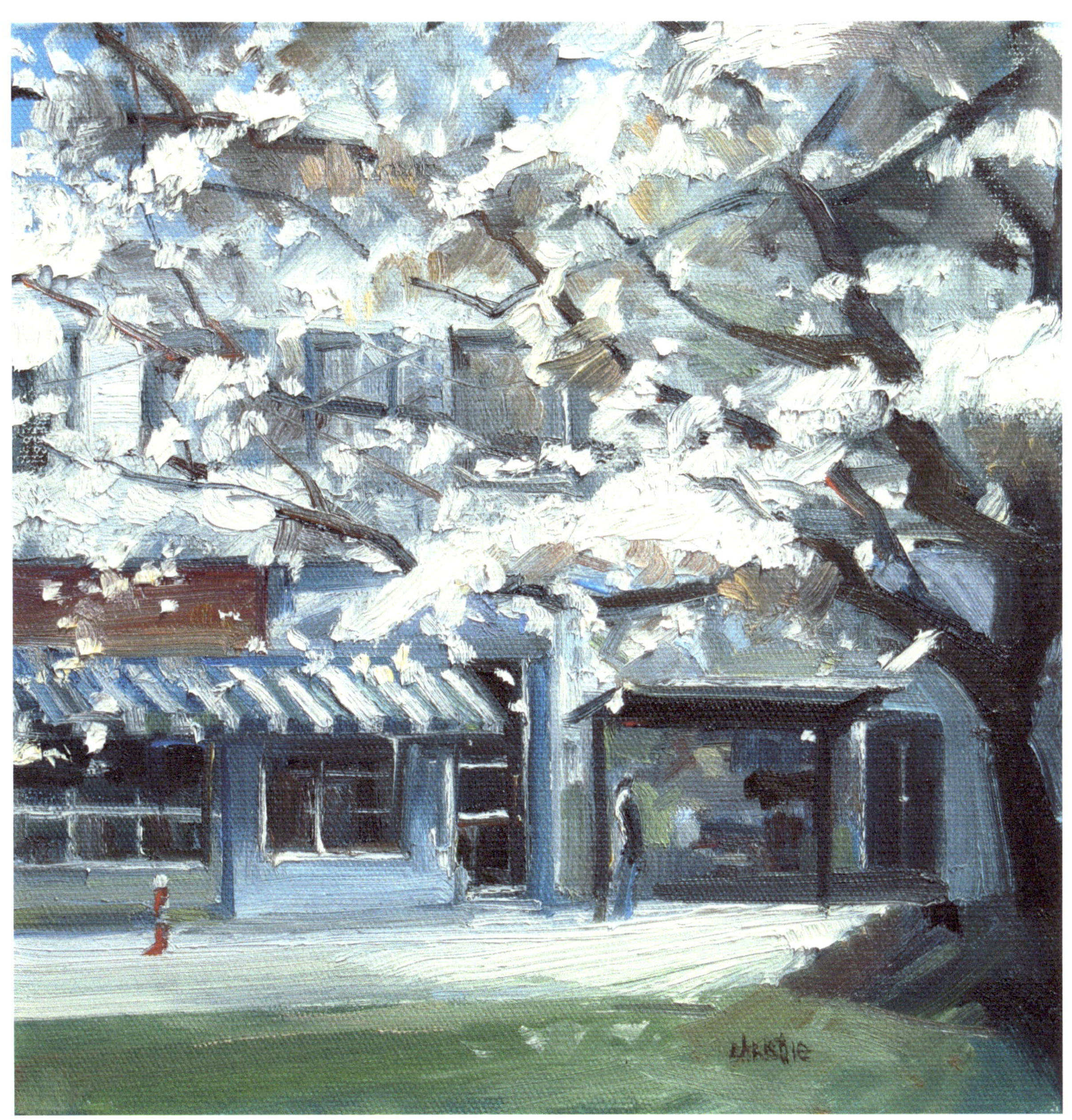

Tolliday on Granville

Oil on canvas. 10" x 10"
2014

Our relationship and intimacy have grown through our long distance communication but in needing to remember someone recently, I noticed that long-distance communication leaves only the abstraction of the relationship. The feeling and the impression. The attachment is true and deep but unsatiated, unanchored and aimless.

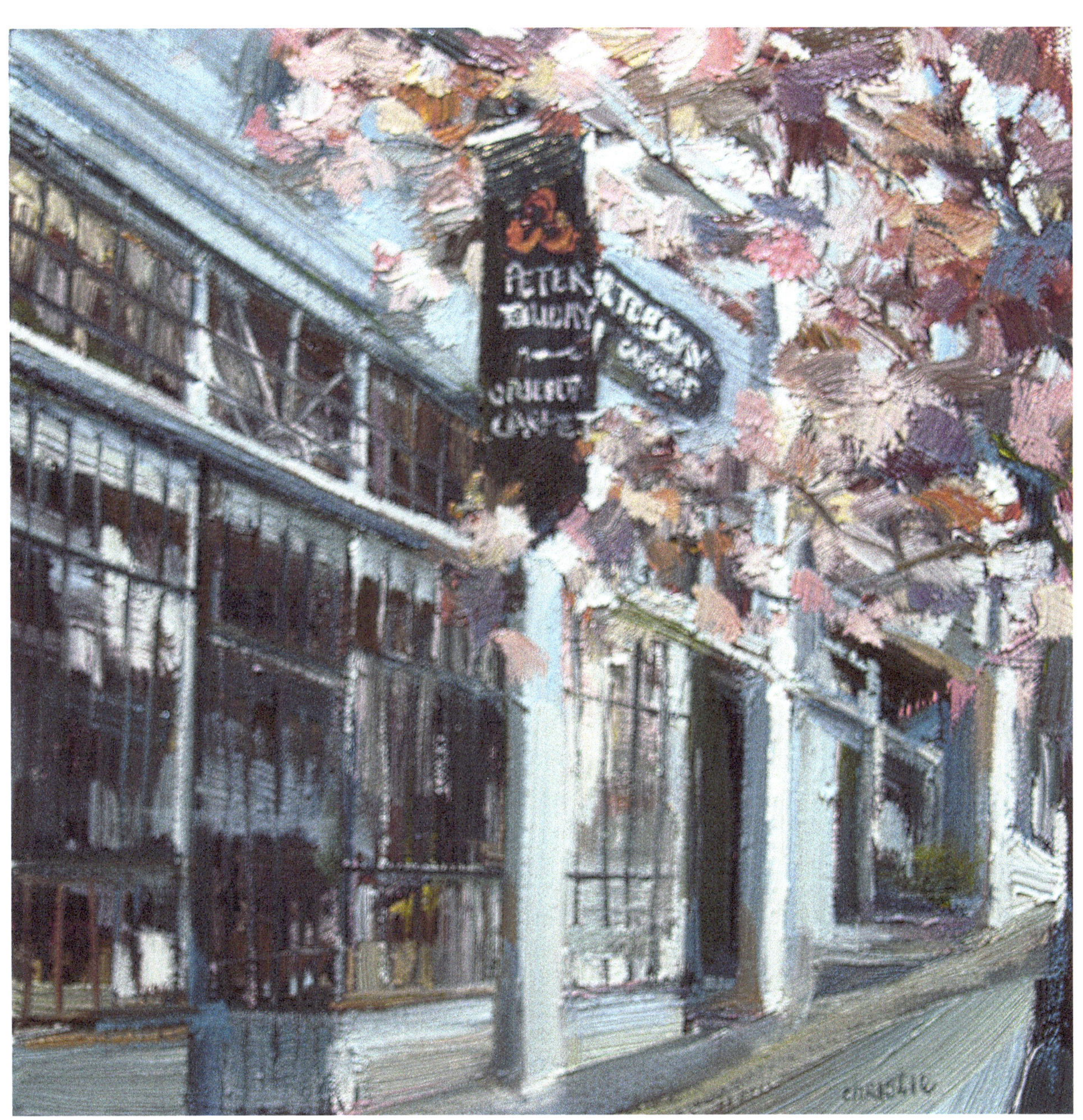
PETER
christie

Burnaby Side Street

Oil on canvas. 10" x 10"

2015

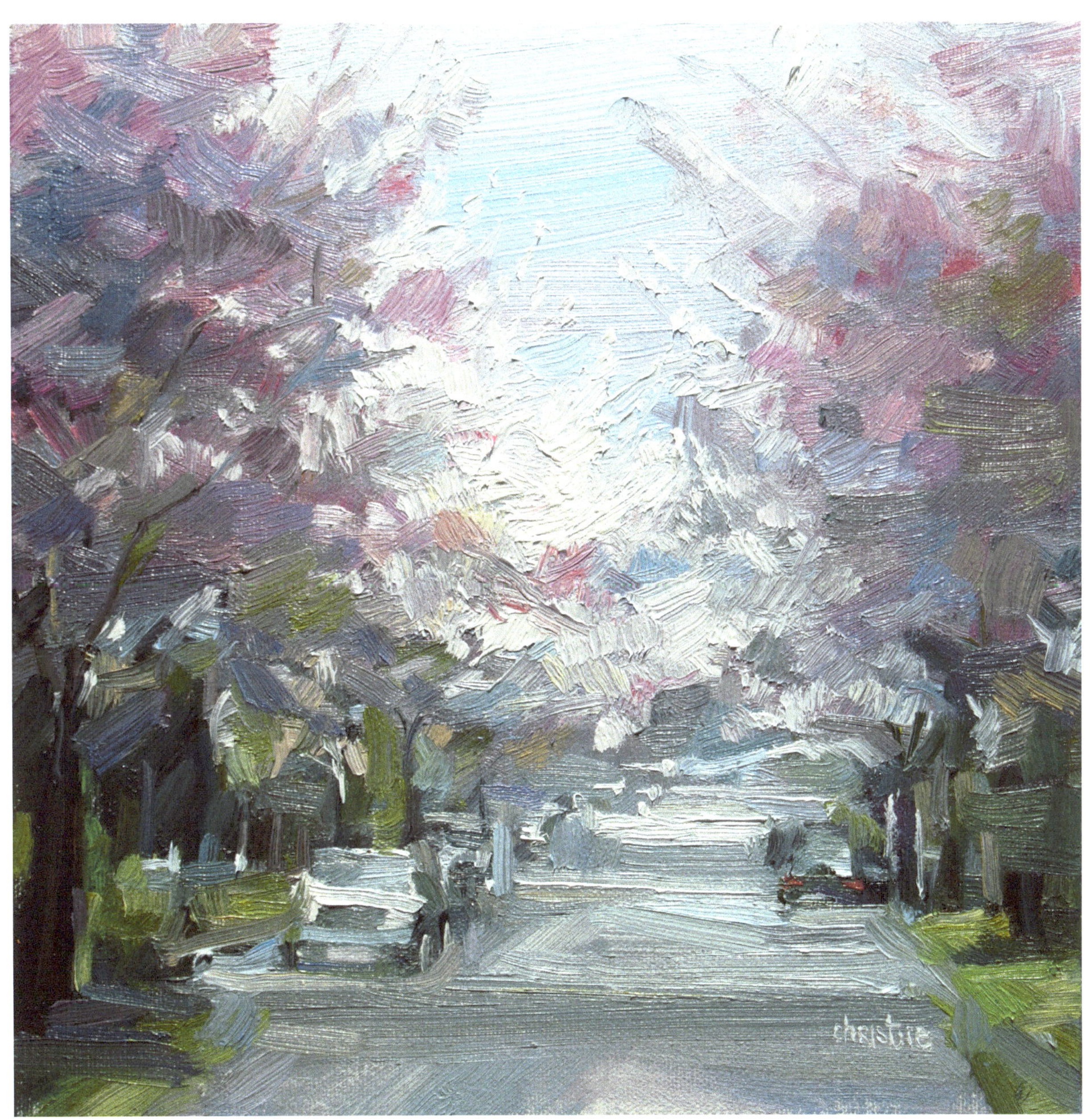
christie

Downtown from Grandview

Oil on canvas. 10" x 10"

2013

My last trip home after 9 years away was startling. Streets and buildings appeared somewhat familiar but not the topography, long adapted to provide for the people present.

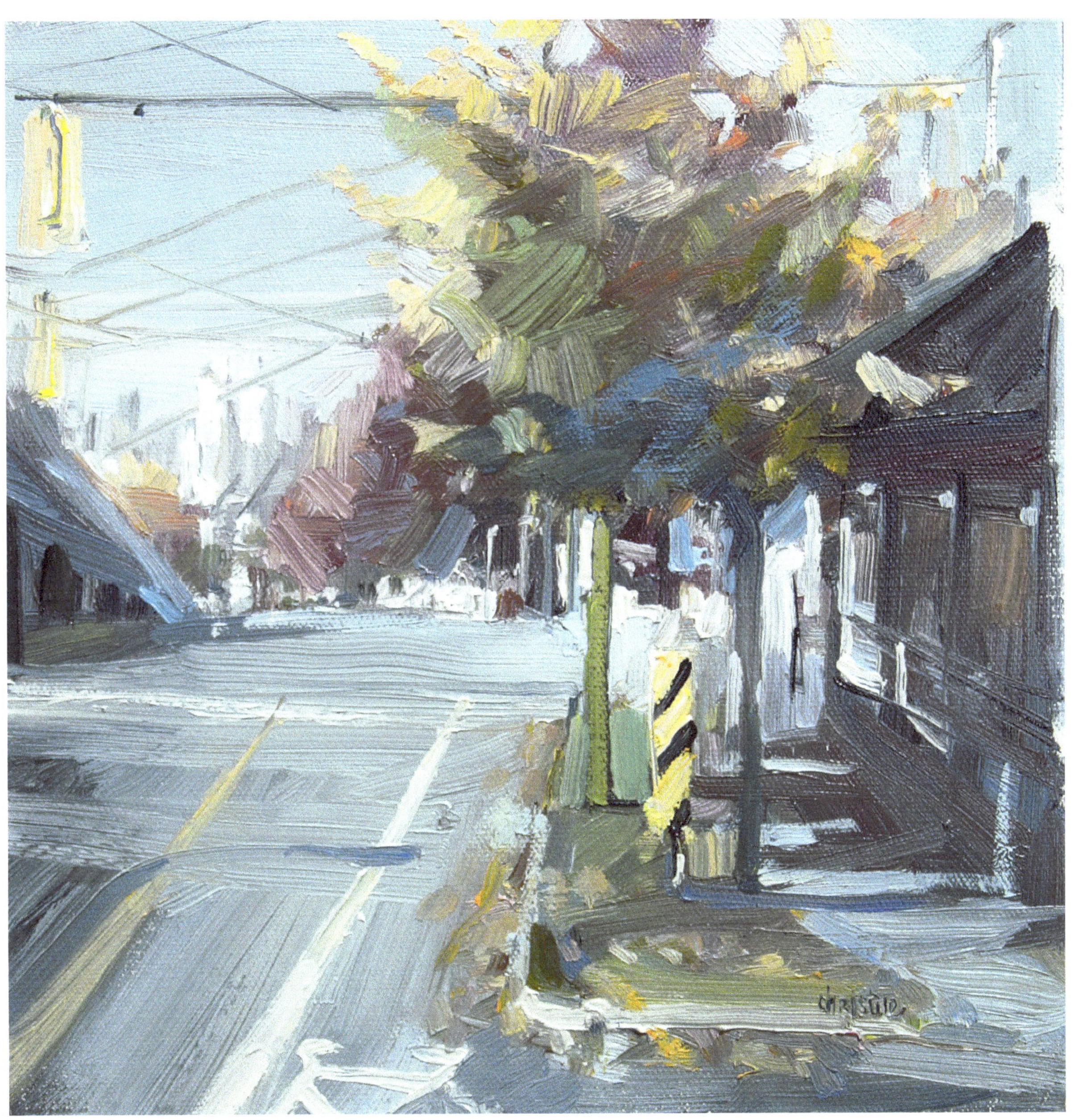

First Days of Spring

Oil on canvas. 10" x 10"

2014

We drove the perimeter of the country, sometimes following the breadcrumbs of memories to ghosts or places that simply didn't exist anymore.

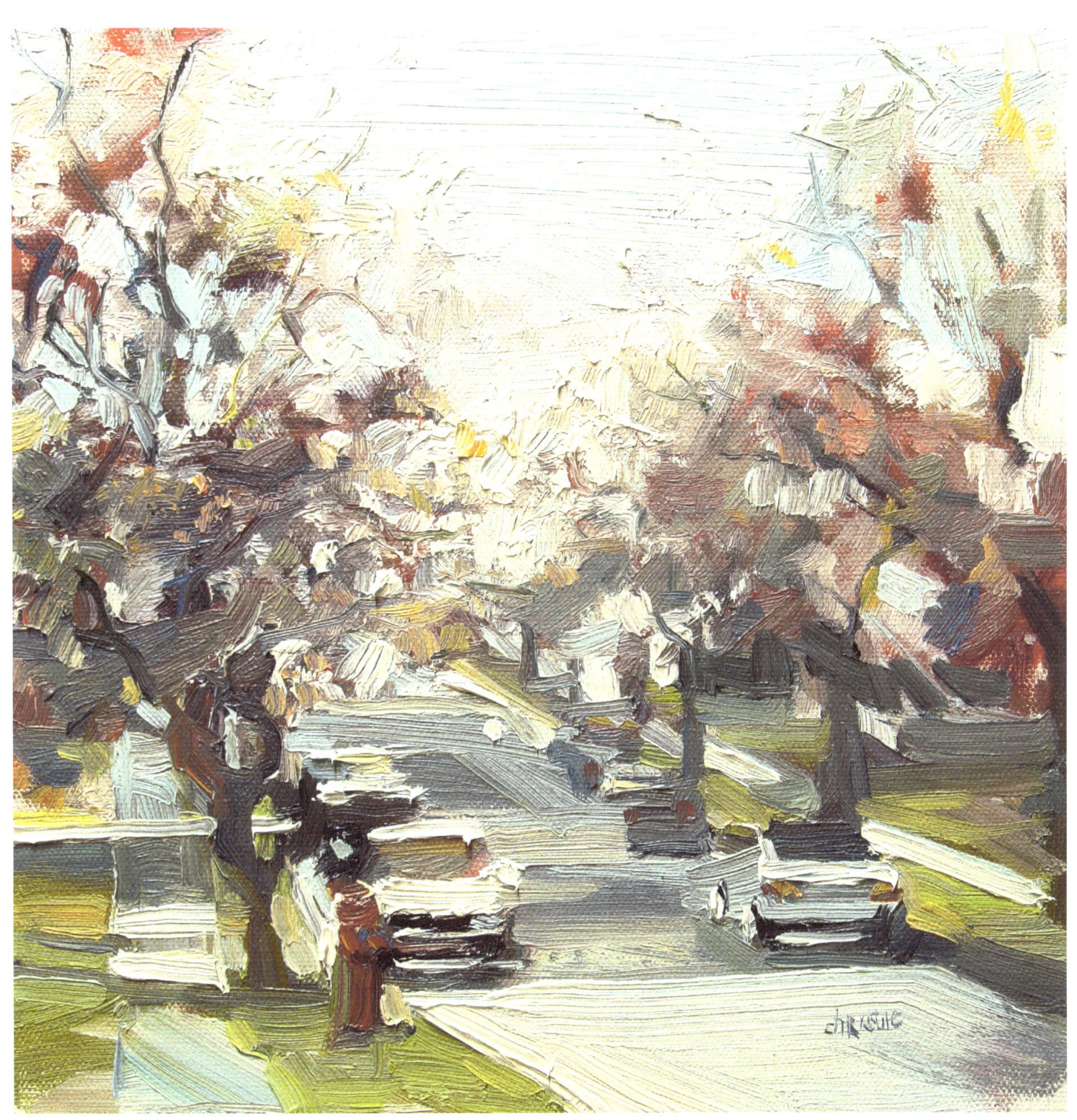

Coal Harbour Transformed
Oil on canvas. 30" x 30"
2015

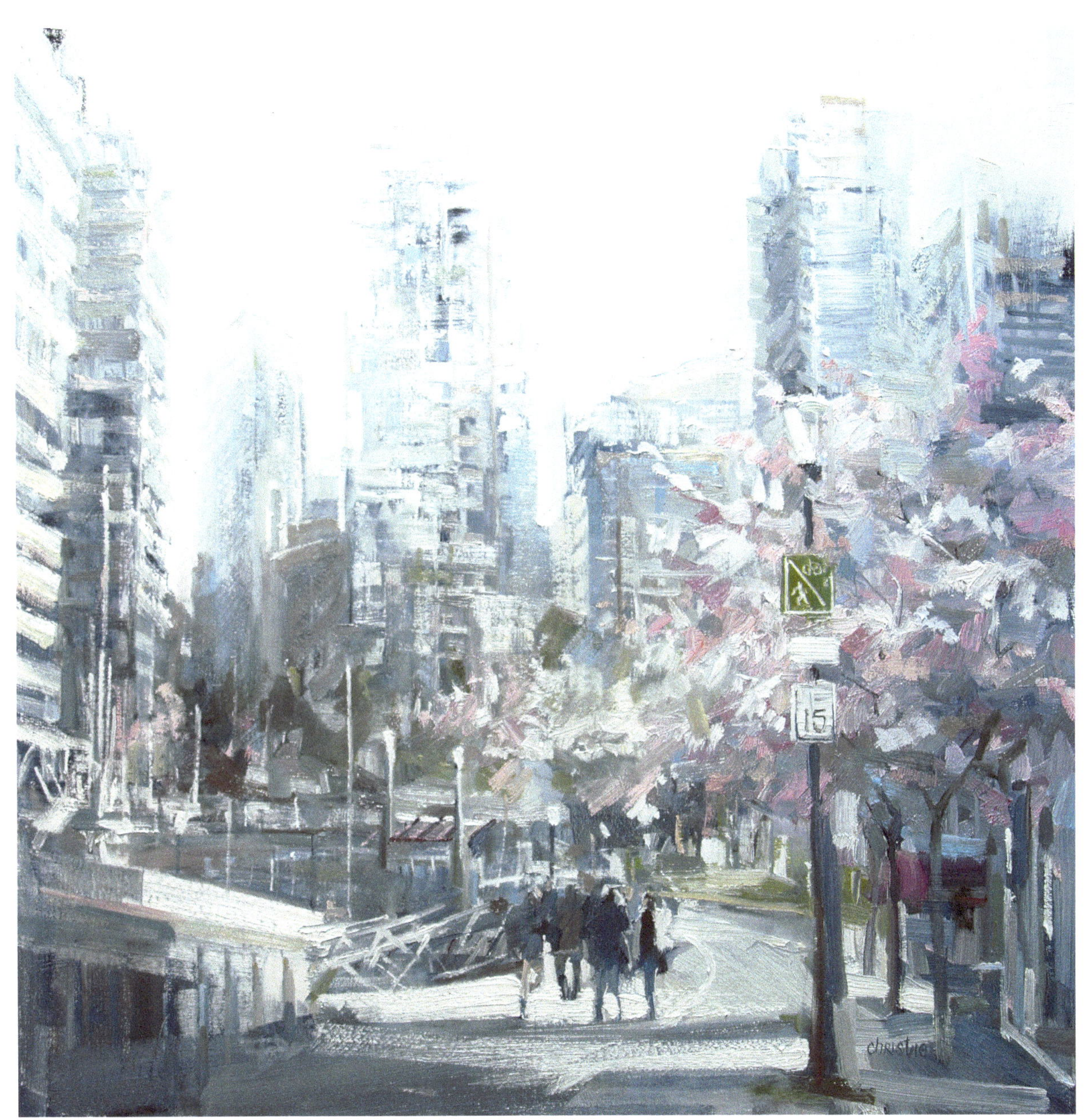
15
christie

Spring

Oil on canvas. 10" x 10"

2015

In losing confidence in my memory and to understand that if the familiar spaces of the city changed beyond recognition that the memories that only they triggered were probably already forgotten, my identity shattered.

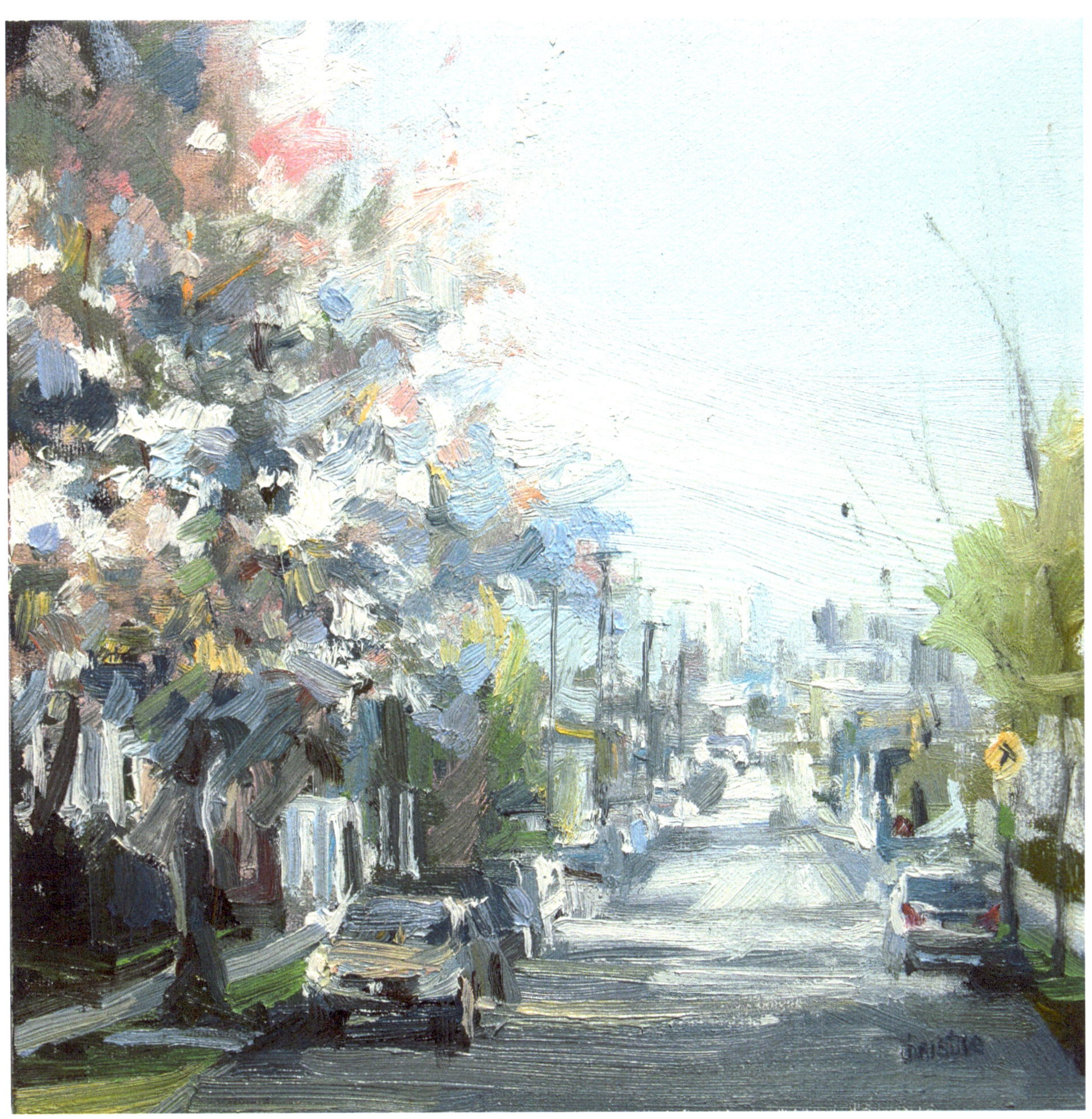

8.35am

Oil on canvas. 24" x 24"

2014

When spaces in our urban become places, they offer us the potential to create memories and these places, special and important, bear witness to our memories and the people in them.

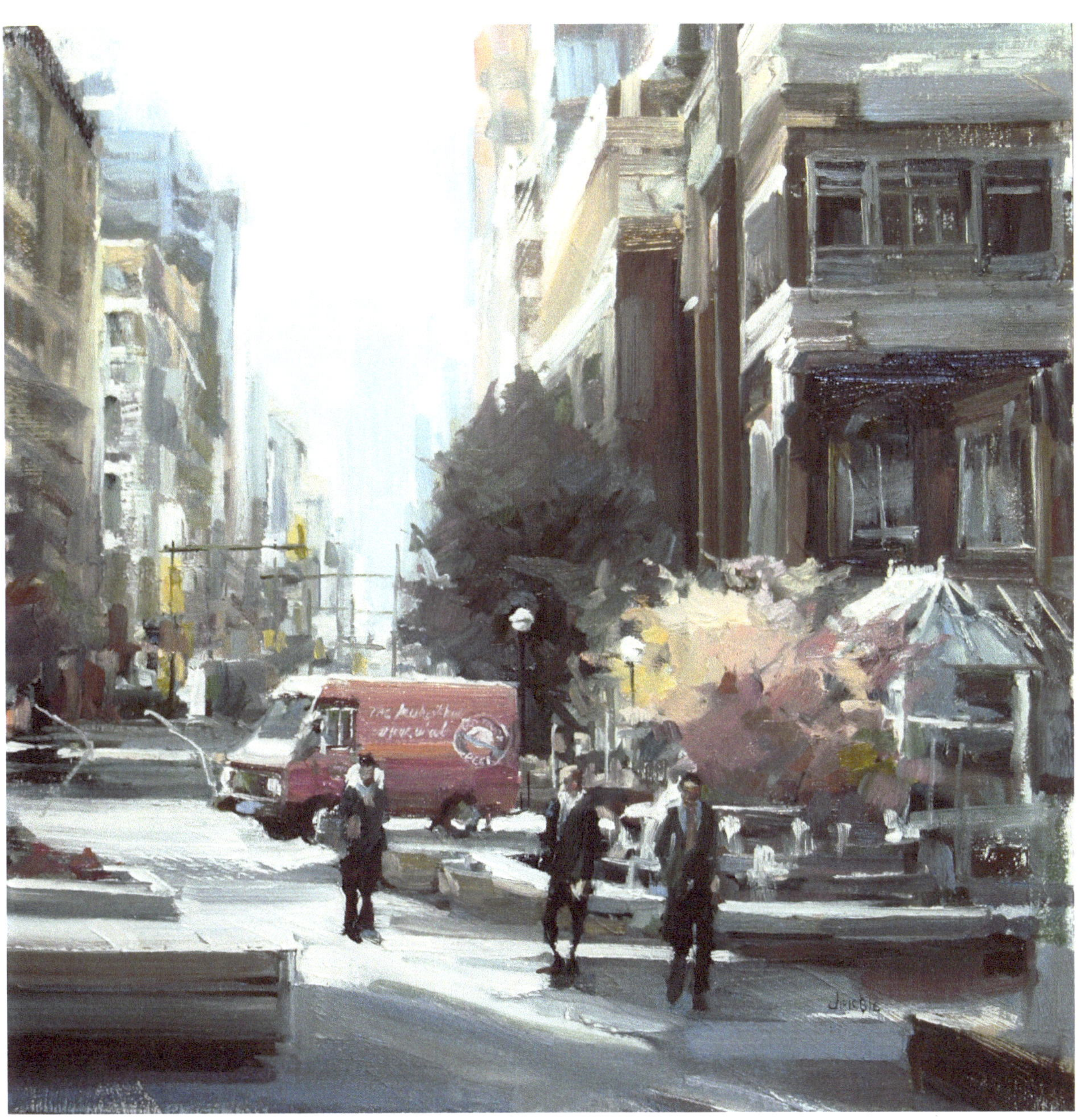

When Giants Sleep
Oil on canvas. 10" x 10"
2018

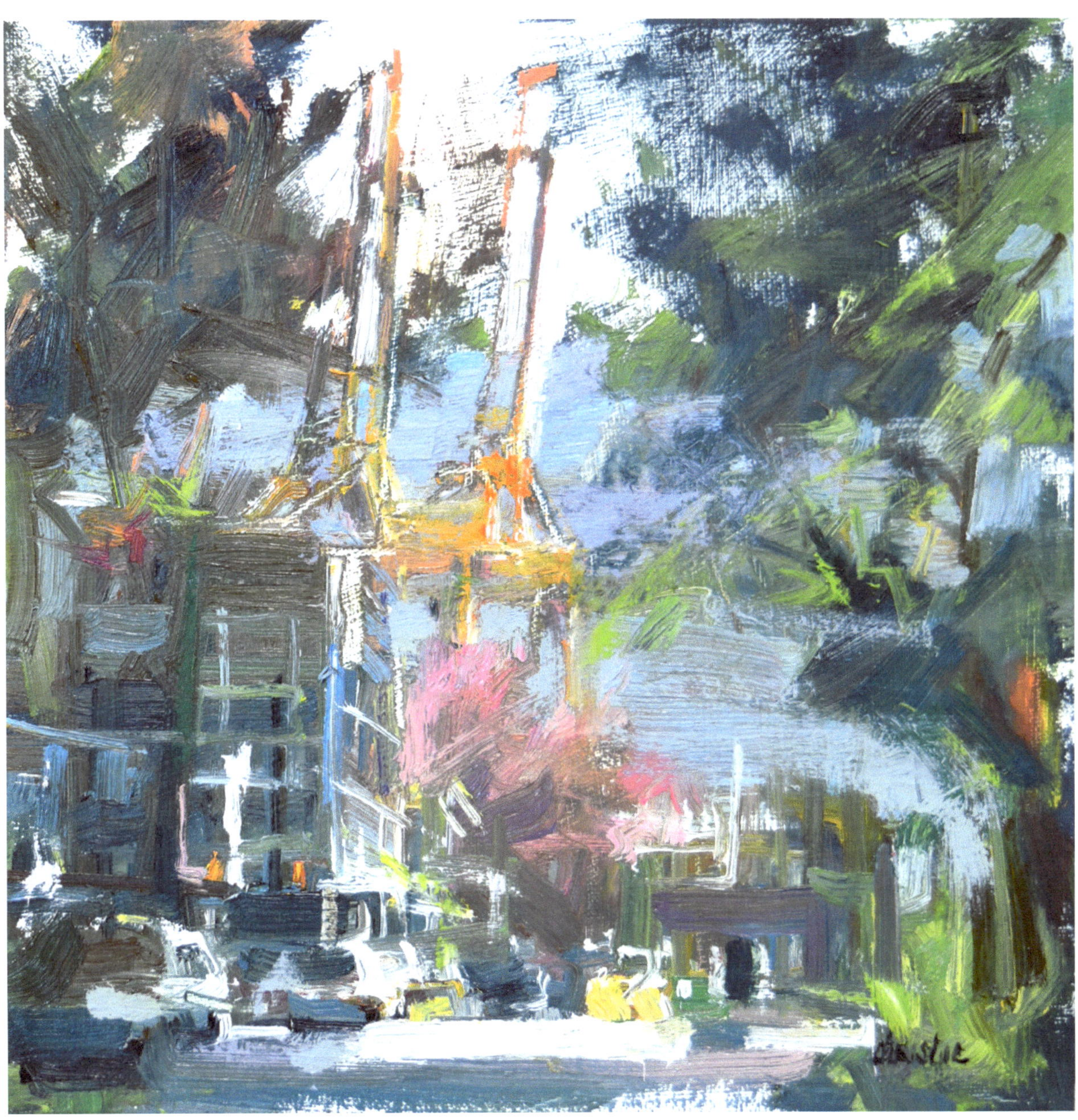

East Pender Blossoms
Oil on canvas. 10" x 10"
2014

It is then appropriate to support a book of intimate Cherry Blossom paintings with thoughts of my grandmothers. The grand dames in a little girls life. One teaching warmth and love and the other a warrior, taller and more resilient every year and who I imagine showing the places that the blossoms create and her saying 'Oh Lee, isn't it wonderful!'

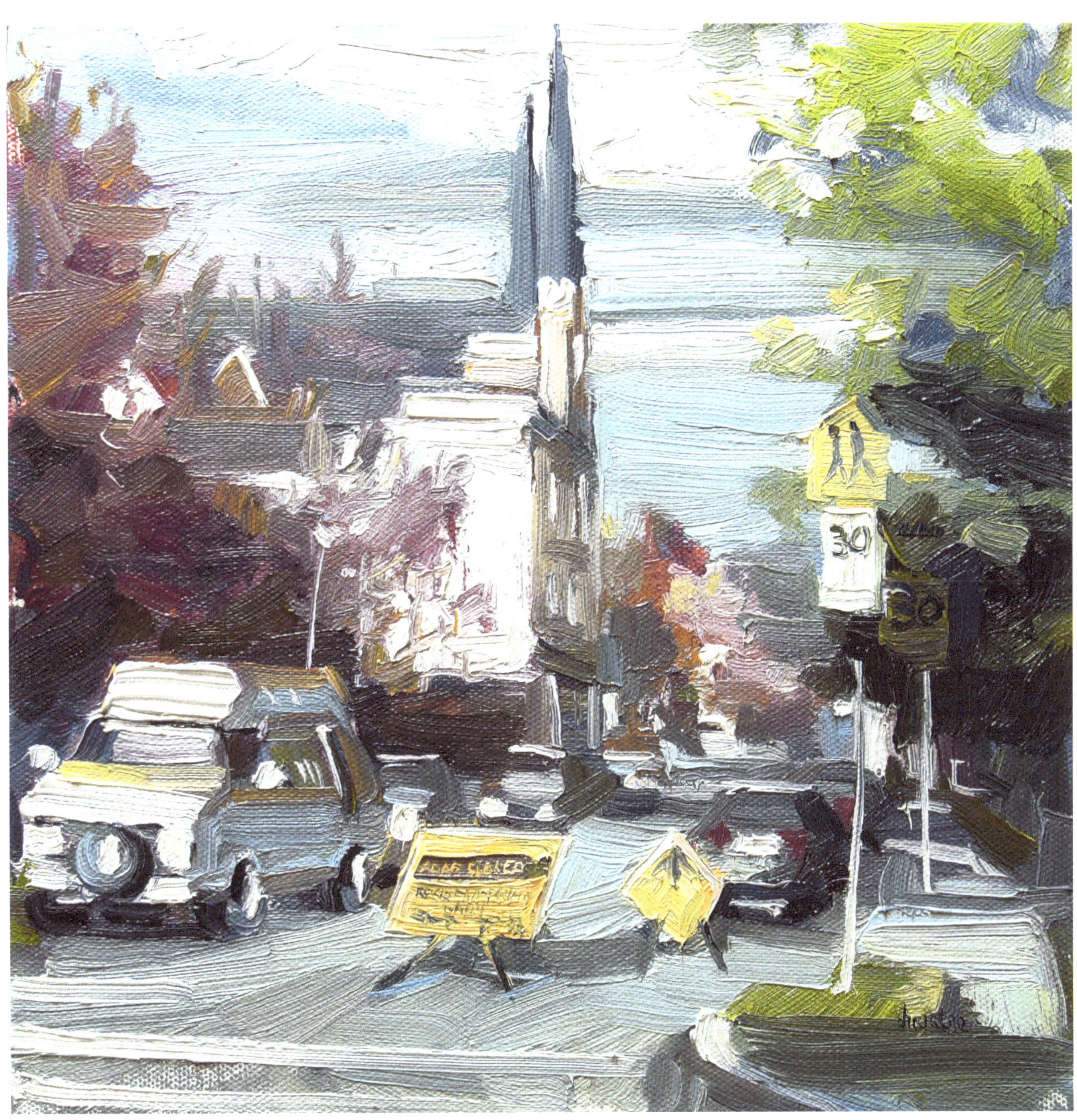

30
30

Sundays

Oil on canvas. 10" x 10"

2013

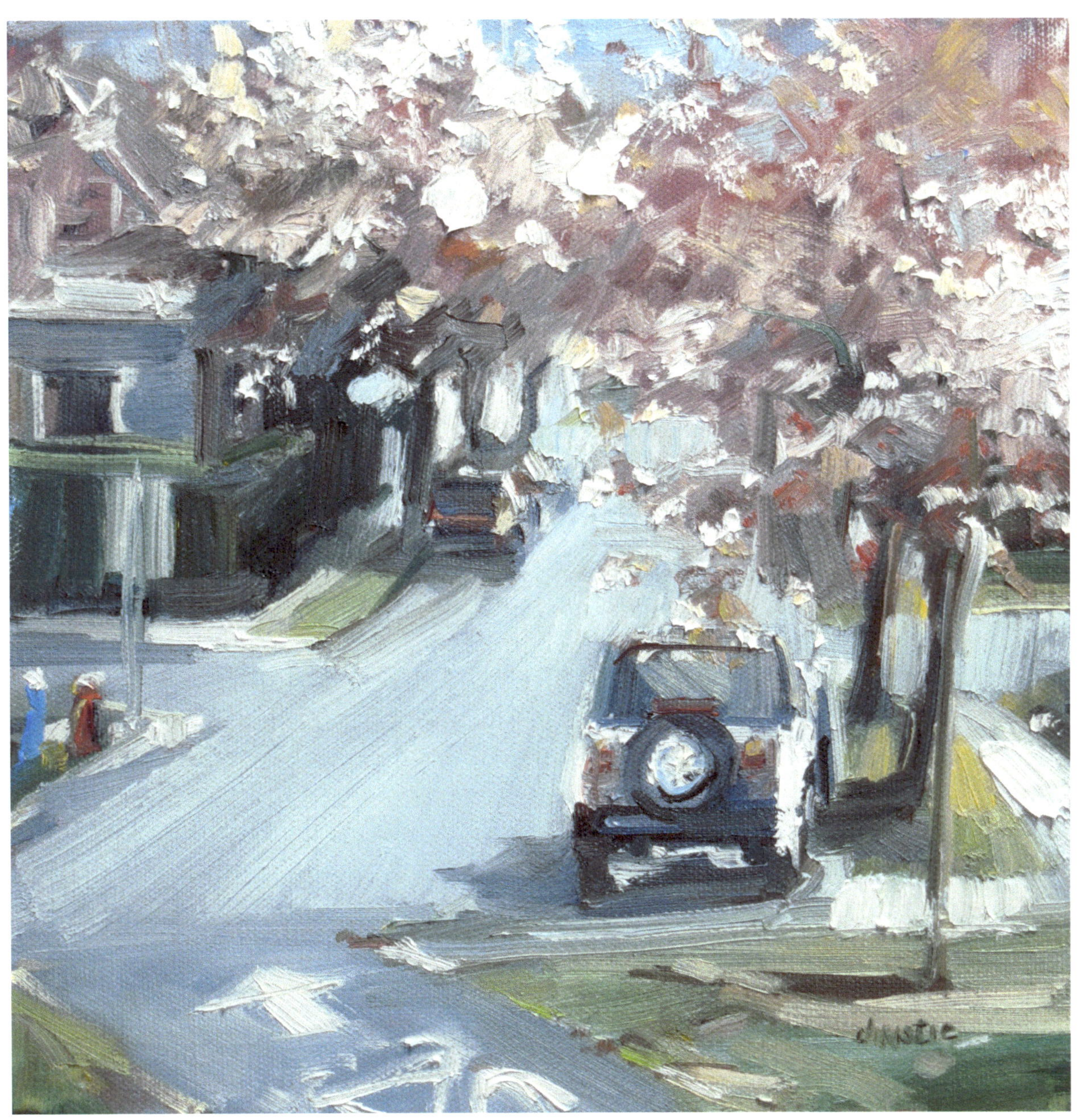

Marshmallowed

Oil on canvas. 24" x 24"

2016

Our evening walks were slow but newsy with our pace recommended by the pull of the stitches. In the lull of the conversation the small figure hunched over her flower bed caught my eye. Her quick hands wove through the soil. I didn't notice any potting mix or little plastic containers holding colourful promises of the season ahead and I wondered when last I had seen someone weeding instead of planting in the endless pursuit of a garden for the season.

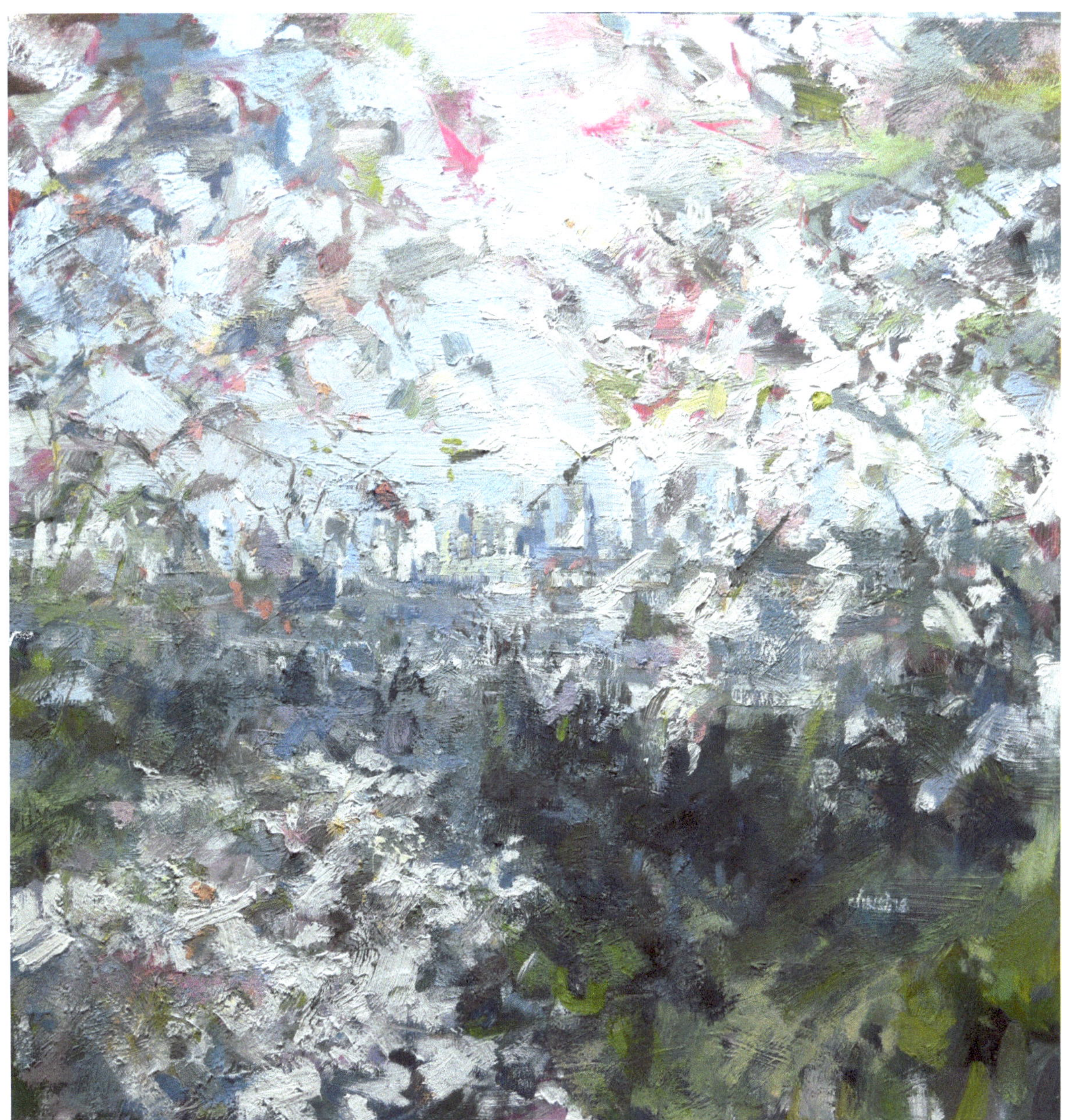

Downtown Woodland Spring

Oil on canvas. 10" x 10"

2014

The fragrant pink petal canopy kept the evening sunshine off her neck as did the floppy, big rimmed garden hat that gave me a little glimpse of the grey underneath.

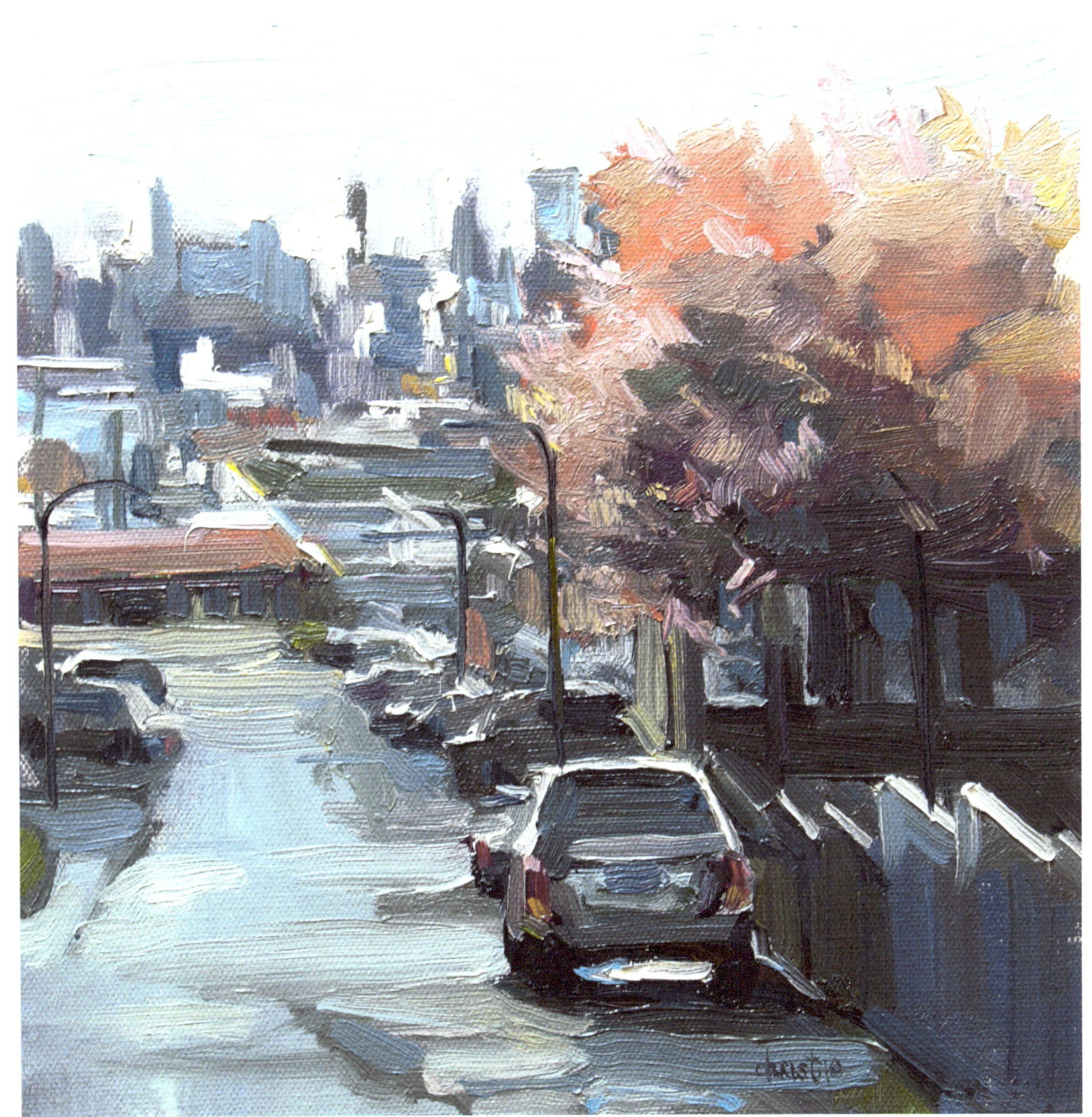
christie

Secluded Strathcona
Oil on canvas. 10" x 10"
2015

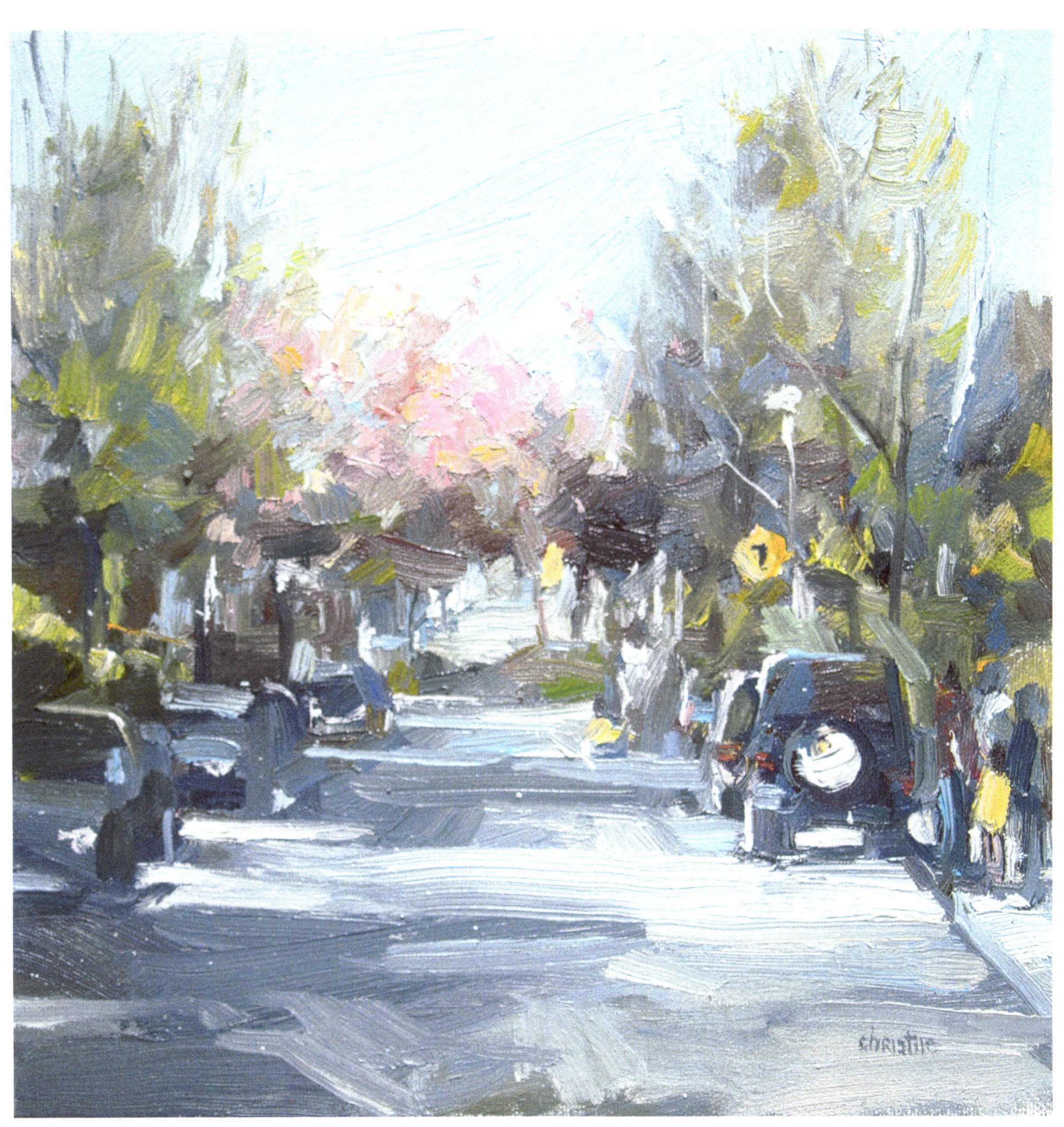
christie

Kitsilano Spring

Oil on canvas. 10" x 10"

2013

The small figure next to her mirrored her actions perfectly. He lifted his head as we passed and after a imperceptible pause to look at his face, I turned back to my conversation 'Spaces becoming places and new memories of grandmothers on warm summer's evenings'

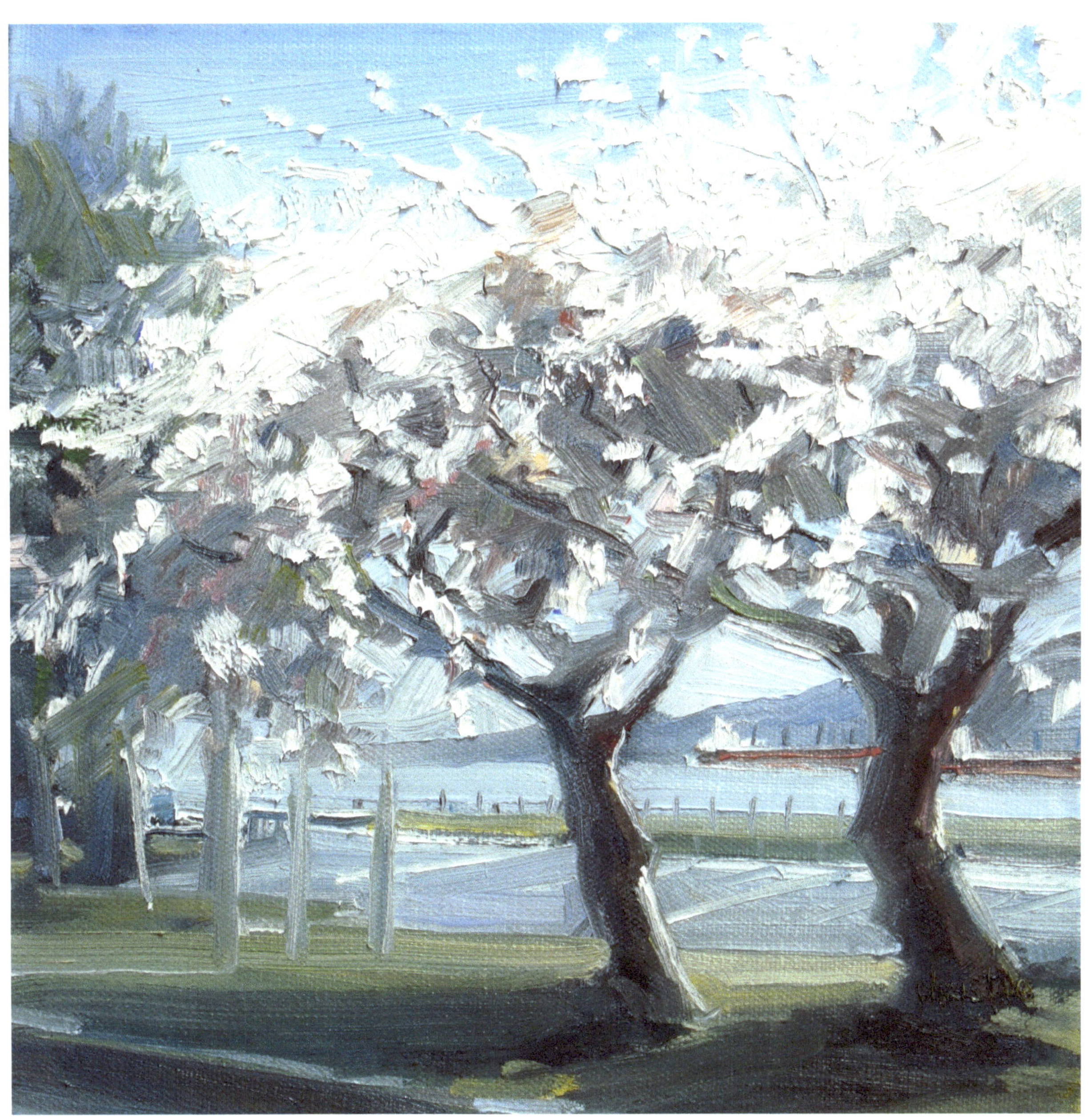

Station

Oil on canvas. 30" x 48"

2015

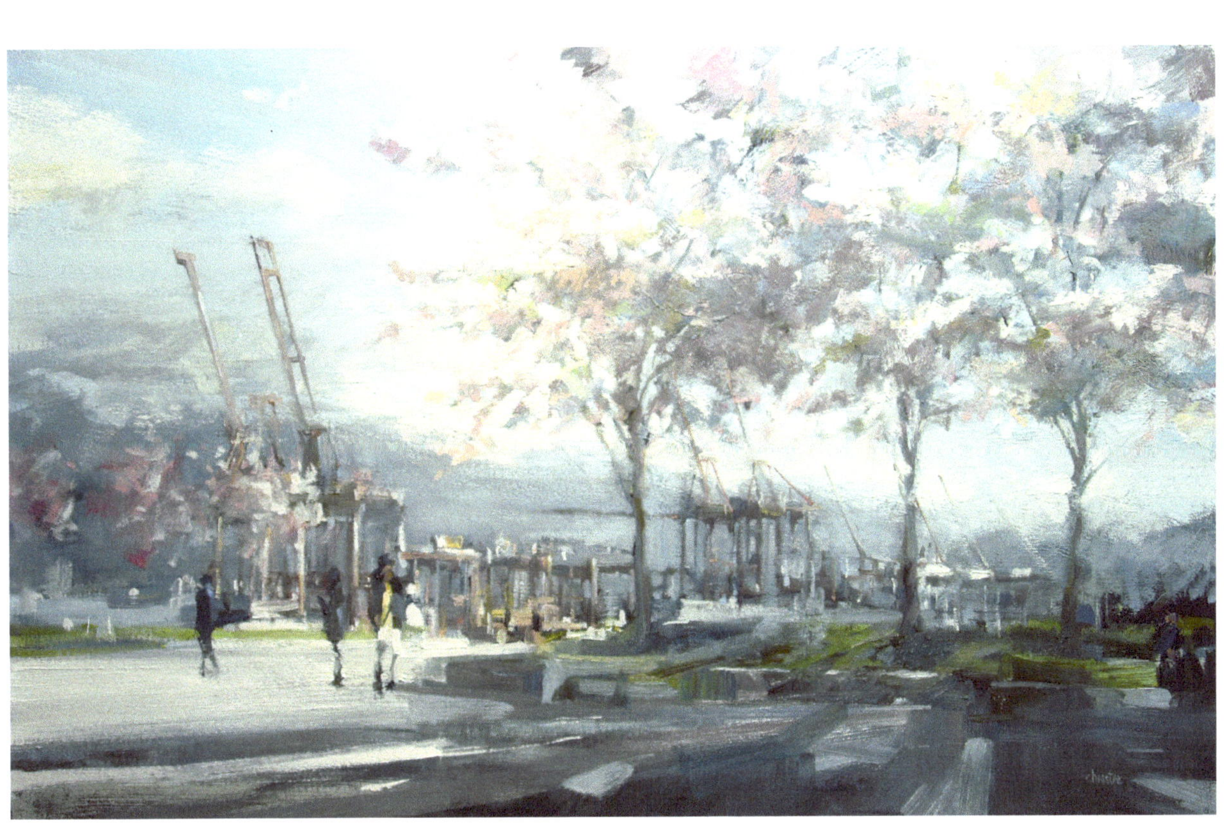

www.ingramcontent.com/pod-product-compliance
Lightning Source LLC
LaVergne TN
LVHW070138110826
845147LV00002B/278
* 9 7 8 1 7 7 5 0 6 3 4 0 7 *